PRAISE FOR *FAT SHAME*

"*Fat Shame* simplifies the complicated relationship between women and their bodies. Nicole shines needed light on a culture obsessed with weight and offers a realistic portrayal of the frustrations regarding size acceptance. *Fat Shame* is a must-read for anyone who looks in the mirror and doesn't love the person they see."

—Dr. David Friedman
TV & Radio Health Expert and Award-Winning #1 Best-Selling
Author of *Food Sanity: How to Eat in a World of Fads and Fiction*

9 Steps
to Find Your
Happiest Weight

HAVE YOU EVER FELT LIKE YOUR SKIN WAS STRETCHED TOO TIGHT ON YOUR BODY?

HAVE YOU TRIED EVERY DIET ONLY TO END UP HEAVIER THAN WHEN YOU STARTED?

Maybe the issue isn't inside your body but rather the way you perceive your body. Download my free guide (fatshame.com) "9 Steps to Find Your Happiest Weight." I look forward to hearing from you on your journey. Remember to trust the process and yourself!

For more tips, follow me

🐦 nicolemotivate 📘 nicolemotivates 📷 nicolemotivates

or go to my website to get in touch:

www.fatshame.com

NEW!

KETO CLEANSE

21-Day
Body
Makeover

JUMPSTART YOUR
WEIGHT LOSS
WITH THE 21-DAY
KETO CLEANSE

You can learn more about the
cleanse on my website:
www.fatshame.com

SHAME

DITCH THE SHAME, GET CONFIDENT, AND CLAIM THE LIFE YOU DESERVE

NICOLE BLACK

Editorial work and production management by Eschler Editing

Cover design by Laura Duffy

Interior design by Michelle Nelson

Published by Whole Beauty Press LLC

www.fatshame.com

ISBN 978-1-7327397-4-1

For Judy—

*Thank you for encouraging me
not to be silent.*

CONTENTS

Introduction 1

Chapter 1: The Truth about Fat Shaming 7

Chapter 2: It's an Inside Job.. 23

Chapter 3: Getting through the Dark Times 39

Chapter 4: Body Armor and Boundaries 57

Chapter 5: Healing Body Dysmorphia........................... 77

Chapter 6: Giving Up the Victim and Blame Game........ 95

Chapter 7: The Road to Happiness 111

Chapter 8: You Are Beautiful! 123

Benediction—My Vision for You 137

Acknowledgments 139

About the Author 147

INTRODUCTION

"You're fat," my very tiny, very short Italian grandmother said to me one day. I was twelve and just entering puberty at the time. And I wasn't "fat." I just wasn't as skinny as she was. But I was too young to understand that her comment had nothing to do with me and everything to do with her own insecurities. Her words wounded me just as deeply as a sharp knife.

I won't say that her comment was the sole reason for the body dysmorphia that plagued me for many years, but it certainly didn't help. My weight was like a ride on a towering roller coaster. I was thin for a while. Then chunky. Then thin (or almost thin) again. Eventually I made it all the way to morbidly obese, tipping the scales at 225 pounds on my 5'1" frame. But the truth is that even when I was a size four, I didn't feel thin or beautiful on the inside.

What I learned is that it doesn't matter how much you weigh. If you don't love yourself for who you are, it won't matter whether you weigh four hundred pounds or eighty pounds. You can be thin on the outside but feel huge and ugly on the inside—or you can be overweight on the outside but feel beautiful and thin on the inside.

And the inside is what really counts. Sure, we all want to be physically healthy, and obesity certainly isn't healthy. But when you truly learn to love yourself as you are, it's actually easier to be physically healthy. The love you feel for yourself causes you to *want* to take care of your body, and the person on the outside begins to reflect the person you've cultivated on the inside.

Unfortunately, many obstacles on the inside can block you from the self-love you deserve. Because of that, you can find the best diet plan known to humankind, but as soon as you get emotionally triggered—often by fat shaming from someone else or even from yourself—the plan flies right out the window.

That's why this isn't a diet book. It isn't about nutrition, fitness, or even about losing weight. It's about helping you embrace your uniqueness and develop an internal framework that will stay strong no matter what you weigh and no matter what anyone says *to* you or *about* you.

For me, the journey to building that strong internal framework involved learning who I was deep inside. That life-changing self-exploration included meditation, psychology, yoga, Rolfing™ Structural Integration, ending my marriage, and most of all, learning how to be single and happy without depending on anyone or anything.

Here's the truth, because I want to be 100 percent transparent with you: I'm no longer overweight. But I didn't lose the weight by dieting and exercise. When I was a hundred pounds heavier than I am now, I tried fasting, working out, and everything else I could think of, but nothing was sustainable.

I lost weight, but I always gained it back. I even got to a point where I was suicidal.

I felt like I was a caterpillar, slowly stuffing myself until I was encased in a cocoon. After I started seeing some of the health risks of my weight, such as high blood pressure, I knew I needed to change or be doomed to a life of huffing and puffing up a short flight of stairs. So I opted for gastric sleeve surgery.

Today, I'm happy with who I am, and people are shocked when they learn that I was once one hundred pounds heavier. I always tell them that if I was going to lie about something, it wouldn't be to make up a story about being overweight!

Let me be clear, however: in no way am I advocating surgery! I still consider it to be a last resort. Yes, the surgery helped me become thinner and physically healthier, but it didn't get rid of the self-loathing or body dysmorphia that still existed inside me from all the years of trauma and fat shaming. So the real work began *after* the surgery. That's when I began to truly heal and love myself. Over time, I unraveled my cocoon to slowly and carefully emerge as a butterfly.

I'm still a work in progress, and my life is far from perfect. But it's also far from where it was when I began this process. I'm convinced that if you follow the principles in this book, you can significantly improve the quality of your life, too.

Is This Book for You?

I believe this book can help you if:

- You've been plagued by fat shaming from others as well as your own inner voice;

- You're overweight and have spent years yo-yo dieting without feeling any better about yourself;
- You don't know if you can love yourself unless you lose weight;
- You want to feel better about yourself and your body, but you don't know how to do it;
- You've experienced trauma that keeps you stress eating;
- You're tired of dieting and want to just accept yourself as you are; and/or
- You want to diet again but feel like you need to deal with your inner pain in order to be successful this time around.

As I've said, what this book *won't* do for you is provide you with a diet plan or give you tips on how to use your willpower to stop overeating. These pages go deeper than that. They speak to the root core of what keeps so many stuck in self-destructive patterns. That may or may not involve losing weight for you. But I'm less concerned about that than I am the quality of your life on a deeper, inner level.

Here's what you'll learn as you continue reading:

- How to protect yourself against the projections and fat shaming of others;
- How to return to neutral when others push your buttons;
- How to spot your personal rock bottom and stop self-loathing in its tracks;
- How to stop giving your power away;
- How to give up the victim/blame game;
- How to cultivate self-forgiveness;
- How to create happiness and joy from the inside out;

- How to love yourself for who you are;
- And more.

Thank you for going on this journey with me. My hope is that it will help you see yourself with new, more loving eyes—regardless of the number on the scale, the size of the clothes you wear, or what anybody else says about you.

chapter one

THE TRUTH ABOUT
FAT SHAMING

*Believe nothing, no matter where you read it or who has
said it, not even if I have said it, unless it agrees with your own
reason and your own common sense.*
—Buddha

I became all too familiar with the phrase *you're fat*, which
was repeated to me countless times by both strangers
and people I knew. They would say it as if it were some grand
revelation or a secret only they could disclose. Sometimes I
wanted to cry in response. Other times I wanted to retort,
"Wow, do you have good eyesight! Stevie Wonder can see *that*."

I wish I could say I developed a thick skin and that none of
the comments and jokes ever got to me or made me angry. But
far too often, the words penetrated, leading me down the dark
pathway toward depression—partially because the fat shaming
seemed to follow me everywhere for more than thirty years.

When I turned forty, for example, I decided to become a
Pilates teacher, but halfway through my training, someone
"helpfully" informed me, "You should be thin if you want to
teach Pilates." I responded that I was healthy on the inside,

but comments like that made me believe that no one would want to learn Pilates from me. It didn't even register in my mind until years later that not everybody who comes to learn Pilates is thin.

When I was twenty-five years old, I was walking down a busy street, insecure about the extra thirty pounds I'd packed onto my petite frame. Someone rolled down a window and yelled out to me, "Hey, fatty, Jenny Craig is right down the street!" They didn't even know my name, so why should I care what they thought about me? Yet, deep down, I did care.

As the car sped away, the tears started to roll down my cheeks, and I could feel my fists clench. Although I've never been a violent person, I wanted to punch something.

Fast forward to age thirty-seven. I was at a Bastille Day picnic in the middle of July. That's the day I made the decision to focus on losing weight. By that time, I weighed about 225 pounds.

It was a hot day, and I felt fat, alone, and out of place as one of the only Americans at the French picnic. All the same, I resolved to have a good time and was enjoying my Diet Coke, smiling and talking to people I had never met before. A man I didn't know started speaking to me. "So what brings you to this party? Who are you with?"

I pointed across the lawn. "I'm the wife of that fine French gentleman across the way."

The man started to laugh uncontrollably to the point that he almost fell off the picnic bench. When he composed himself, he said, "You must be mistaken! No man that good-looking would ever be married to a *thing* that looks like *you*."

THE TRUTH ABOUT FAT SHAMING

I was dumbfounded. I wasn't a *thing*! How could one human being say something so cruel to another human being—a stranger, no less? I wish I could have stood up and left, but it was as if my feet were encased in cement. I also wish I could say it stopped there, but it didn't. This man was unrelenting in his taunts, and I was left speechless.

Eventually, another person at the picnic told him to lay off. "Yes, that man over there *is* her husband. Leave her alone." But he wouldn't.

I was determined not to cry in front of him, but my eyes brimmed with tears. Then my husband walked over. He never said a word to the man who was so horrible to me, but he did ask if I wanted to leave. My former spouse had the uncanny ability to let things roll off his back, so he just asked me, "Why do you care what that man thinks about you?" I couldn't answer him. He pointed out that it was unlikely I'd ever see this person again. He was right, of course, but at that time, it wasn't as easy as that for me.

I'll never forget the feeling of receiving that man's cruelty. It was as if he had some vendetta against fat chicks and was taking it out on me personally.

The situation at the picnic brought me right back to an experience I had when I was twenty-six. I weighed just more than 125 pounds, and I thought I looked good. I wasn't perfect, because no one is, but I felt good about myself and my body. I was wearing a cute size four skirt with a little white sweater and black high heels.

A man I'd never seen before and would never see again walked up to me at a club and told me I was fat. He said it with such disdain that I physically recoiled. The sneer on his face and the darkness in his eyes led me to believe that I must actually *be* fat. He was that convincing.

Unfortunately, I was young and gullible enough that I didn't realize men say things out of anger toward women in general. I didn't know how to *not* take it personally.

In another incident, I owned a French bakery and was stunned during an exit interview with an employee. He thought we needed to limit the amount of calories each person was allowed to purchase. Only the "fat people"—people he thought were fat or should be on a diet—would be subject to the restriction. It was a shocking and ridiculous notion, but it fed into my own self-loathing and left me feeling rotten.

A customer even told me once that I'd know how to give good customer service if I were thin. What? Even the reviews people posted online often revolved around my weight.

Perhaps one of the most painful times was when my husband shamed me. I had been trying to lose my pregnancy weight after our baby was born, but nothing seemed to work. I tried fasting and working out. The one thing I wasn't doing was sleeping enough. In order to lose weight, you need to sleep. But I was too busy running around after a baby and a husband who was repulsed by my appearance.

One day, I was sitting on the edge of the bed, and he looked at me in disgust. He placed a hand over my belly and flipped the skin up. "How do you think I could possibly be attracted to *that*?" he said. Wasn't I still the same person on the inside? It was the same area of my body where I had carried our child.

Then there were the heartbreaking times I witnessed others being fat-shamed. I went on a school field trip with my daughter, and the bus driver was overweight. Some of the teenage boys started to make fun of the driver's weight, even planning cruel stunts like asking him to sit in a chair they knew was broken. They said all of this within earshot of the driver.

I was able to speak to the driver one day when all of the children were running around an Indian reservation grabbing souvenirs. He had been a nineteen-year-old with a promising career as a discus thrower—possibly even good enough to qualify for the US Olympic Team. Then his girlfriend got pregnant, and he needed to get a job to take care of his new family. He felt that was the right thing to do. He didn't have many skills and couldn't take the time to go back to college to expand his skillset, so he took the best-paying job he could find, which was driving a bus. Years of sedentary work led to him becoming overweight.

These stories illustrate just a fraction of what those of us who are overweight endure on an almost daily basis.

Why Do People Feel the Need to Shame Others?

People fat-shame for many reasons. They feel bad about themselves, so they lash out at others in order to feel better. It's a classic projection of their own anger, fear, jealousy, or insecurity. It's their personal coping mechanism.

I came to understand this because my own coping mechanism used to be eating. But the people who shame us cope by making other people feel bad. What a terrible way to live—

trying to make themselves feel better by making others feel worse. If you think about it that way, it's easy to have some empathy for people who feel the need to do that.

The truth is, we've probably all inadvertently (or willfully) shamed someone at some point in our lives. Think about the last time a friend of yours got something fabulous, like a new job. What was your reaction? Did you smile and tell her you were excited for her?

I was once able to buy a shiny new BMW. I was so excited and proud that I could finally afford that car, but a friend reminded me that the repair bills would likely be very costly, and that I would no longer have a warranty once the car reached 50,000 miles. "The car will fall apart then, you know," she told me. She could have just as easily said, "I'm so happy for you! I can't wait to go for a spin!" But her jealousy got the better of her.

Since I hadn't yet learned how to deflect the shaming of others, I felt deflated and defeated the next time I hopped into my car. It was so much harder to enjoy the car I loved. Unwittingly, my friend also solidified her negative thought patterns about cars and maintenance. If she ever wanted a car like that for herself, she just made it a lot harder to bring it into her life because she programmed her mind against it.

Shaming others is never a true positive outcome for the person doing the shaming. Like my food addiction, it's a temporary "fix" to a dangerous underlying problem.

But when you're the target of the shaming, it can be very hard to maintain your equilibrium and avoid letting the barbs cut you emotionally. Still, you can get better at letting negative comments roll off your back. I've managed to do it, and I know you can, too.

The truth is that we can't fix anyone else; we can only fix ourselves. So while there's no way to control what others say or do to us, we *can* alter how we react to them. Once you know that people who shame you are simply projecting their own insecurities onto you, you'll recognize that what they say is a result of their own deficiencies. It has nothing to do with you. Let's explore ways that you can recover from the onslaught of someone else's shaming.

Exercise: How to Recover from Shaming

The next time someone shames you, give yourself a moment to recoil. The shaming is often a bit of a shock, so you may need to catch your breath. Here are some steps you can take to recover faster from cruel words:

1. Take slow, deep breaths to slow down your nervous system. Inhale to a count of five, and exhale to a count of five. The slow exhale can be difficult. It might help to form a small circle with your lips, and blow the air out slowly through that circle. Do this as many times as you need in order to slow down your heart rate and begin to feel like yourself again.
2. Don't react verbally! If you feel you can't avoid a reaction, laugh. It will disarm the person. But remember that you can't fix this person. Your goal is to find your own balance.
3. Remind yourself that the individual who spoke unkindly is in pain. They may not even know they're in pain, but deep down, they are.
4. Later, when you're alone, write down how you felt emotionally and in your body as a result of the words. Making note of where you felt it in your body can be helpful

down the road, as you'll begin to see patterns as to how your nervous system responds. You'll also become more accustomed to tuning into your body, and writing down your feelings will help you release them. As much as it might hurt to do this, it will ultimately help you. If you feel the need to cry or punch a pillow, do it! Whatever you do, don't stuff the feelings down. That could easily send you to food, and even if it doesn't, the healthy way to let go of a painful experience is to let your feelings out. You're reaching for your pen rather than a candy bar and giving yourself what you truly need. The longer issues like this linger and fester, the more they become a bigger deal than they deserve to be.

5. While you're writing, ask yourself four questions: (1) *Is what the person said true?* (2) *Is what the person said helpful?* (3) *Is the comment in line with who I am as a person?* (4) *Does this person's opinion truly affect my life?* Chances are the answers to these questions are all *No*. If you get a *Yes* on any of these, double-check yourself. If the comment was helpful, it could be that you learned something valuable about yourself. If that's the case, try not to use it as an excuse to beat yourself up, but simply use it as a way of developing yourself further. If the person's opinion will indeed affect your life, ask yourself in what way. If he/she is a family member, I question how much their opinion must *truly* affect your life. If it's your boss or a colleague, maybe it's time to begin thinking about how you can change jobs. (Don't automatically

tell yourself you won't be able to find another job or that you've invested too much in this job.)

6. Next, sit down and have a talk with yourself; remind yourself that you're unique and inherently lovable. It takes time and practice, but that self-talk will eventually begin to penetrate the habit of self-hatred that may have plagued you for years. Don't give up! Keep combatting that negative voice. Slowly but surely, your loving voice will become louder.

7. Finally, ask yourself, *Who was I before this comment landed on me?* That's what you want to return to. Now that you've allowed your feelings to come out in your journal, affirm to yourself that you'll reset and act as if the comment never came your way. Then close your eyes and imagine that a rush of beautiful white light is coming toward you from above. You can imagine that this light is coming from Spirit, angels, departed loved ones—whatever feels good to you. Allow this light to swirl around you in a spiral that will protect you from the negative energy of others. If you like, allow the heavens to open and shower you with petals from your favorite flower. Know that you are loved regardless of the number on your bathroom scale. You can use this swirl of white-light protection every day if you want to.

The Mirror of Fat Shaming

Those two little words, *you're fat*, reverberated through my head after so many shaming experiences. But what I learned was that even when I wasn't fat on the outside, I had a fat mentality going on inside my head. The scale didn't matter. The size of my clothes had no bearing on how I saw myself. This cycle of self-abuse continued for well more than a decade until I learned how to quiet the destructive voice that liked to take my power away.

It didn't really matter if someone else thought I was fat. I was beating myself up on the inside for not being enough of whatever I thought other people wanted me to be. And the people who shamed me were holding up a mirror to my own inner shame. That was a hard realization, but it was an important one.

The truth is that you're enough today, and you'll be enough tomorrow. And you aren't "too much," either. Like everyone else, you're a work in progress, and there's no one else in the world like you. NO ONE. Never has been, and never will be.

It isn't about being fat or skinny. You're in control of your life, your body, and your choices. No one else gets to dim your light. And in truth, they can't dim your light. Only you can do that if you allow someone else's warped opinion of you to control you. I believe you're stronger than that and deserve better than that. Don't you? Yes, you do! Maybe a part of you doesn't believe that yet, but there's another part of you who knows better. It may be the tiniest whisper in your head right now. You may see this part of you as a miniscule pinpoint of light. But that light can get bigger if you let it. In fact, right now, see if you can grow that light. Can you make it bigger? Can you make that whisper louder? Can you hear the voice of the part of you who loves you unconditionally?

If you can't, keep trying. The more often you open your ears to this part of you, the faster it will begin to drown out the part that's mirrored by the shamers.

Self-love is a lifelong practice, so don't ask yourself to be perfect at it. It's like brushing your teeth. You have to do it daily, and you *will* get better at it. But you'll never be perfect, because none of us are. During the course of reading this book, you'll learn new skills for loving yourself. By the time you finish the last page, you'll already be better at self-love!

Exercise: Anchor within Your Own Self-Love

I have a theme song. That's right—it's a song that I've always loved: Cyndi Lauper's "True Colors." I picked this song because it feels like a pep-talk geared toward finding your own inner beauty and strength. It's about holding yourself in high regard, which is the most important gift you can give yourself. It's about hope and honoring yourself—all the things I wasn't doing for myself when I realized the song should be my theme. (Remember: There's a difference between being an egomaniac and knowing that you deserve all the best life has to offer.)

At first, the song made me feel deeply uncomfortable because I didn't feel that way about myself. Today, that theme song is one of the ways I anchor myself in my self-love. When someone says something unkind, I hear that song in my head. When my old patterns of self-criticism start in on me, I instantly play that song in my head.

Choose your own theme song right now. It can be whatever helps you feel good. It can be instrumental, or it can have lyrics. If it does have lyrics, just make sure those lyrics are uplifting.

Walking Away from Toxic People

It's difficult to walk away from people who don't serve your best interests, especially when they're a big part of your life. These are people who have mastered the art of getting under your skin, and often, they've known you a long time.

Maybe this person constantly points out your flaws, laughs at your mistakes, or insults you in comments that they claim are compliments. You know the ones, like "Wow, you're not as fat as you were the last time I saw you!" Gee, thanks for that. They relish using your insecurities and flaws as a weapon against you. If they know you have some insecurity with the extra skin that hangs under your chin, they'll be sure to point that out. But remember: They're only doing this because of their own fears, jealousies, and insecurities.

Sometimes you have to take steps to let go of people, even if you've been close to them for years. I had to end a relationship with my husband because it had turned toxic for both of us. Of course, you can't always end a toxic relationship. What if the toxic person is your mother or your spouse's father? You can do whatever possible to limit the amount of time you're around this individual, but you may still have to deal with them from time to time.

You could try the direct approach: "I won't be able to be around you anymore if you continue to put me down." Of course, if this person has little self-awareness or some mental illness, he/she may not know how to stop. You may be told that you're wrong or that you're overreacting.

But I strongly urge you to extract yourself from the toxic person if at ALL possible. If you truly feel you can't, practice some of the tips that are listed earlier in this chapter. Begin to disengage from your belief in what this person says to you. See the person for who he is—someone in pain who is deflecting that pain by trying to pass it on to you. It's sad, isn't it?

Use the experience as best you can as an opportunity to grow stronger. Take it as a challenge: "I will stay anchored in my own self-love no matter what this person says, and I will *not* stuff my feelings down with food. I won't tell myself that I can't overcome it. I'll write about how I feel, I'll cry, and/or I'll punch a pillow in order to get my anger and hurt out. Maybe I'll take a boxing or kickboxing class!"

You Are Not Your Shame or Your Body

Just remember that you're so much more than moments of shame. You're so much more than your body. As you age, your body changes and becomes less "beautiful" by society's standards. It happens to everyone, including thin people, and it doesn't make anyone less valuable. Neither does your weight. Whether you weigh eighty pounds or four hundred pounds, you're a worthy, gorgeous, one-of-a-kind human being.

Think about it: Do you love anyone for what they weigh or because of their age? I'll bet you don't. You love them for who they are. And the people who truly love you do so for who you are, not for your age, weight, or anything else having to do with how you look.

This was grilled into me by an employee when I worked in the bakery. He was a high-school surfer dude who sometimes closed the store with me. One of those days, I told him that an old friend of mine wanted to come for a visit. "I can't see her!" I said.

He raised his eyebrows and asked, "Why not?"

"Because look at how fat I am! There's no way she would really want to see me if she knew."

He was puzzled. "Why would someone who's your friend care what you weigh? I don't care what my friends weigh."

When my friend called later to talk about our meeting, I said, "I'm uncomfortable seeing you because I've gained so much weight since you saw me last."

"Nicole, I'm not trying to date you," she said. "I just want to see my friend."

The truth is that people who love you only if you weigh a certain amount aren't worthy of you, are they? Because that makes them superficial people who deserve your pity and your hope that they learn to be more caring. If they aren't any more caring than that toward others, just think how little they must care about themselves. Think about how much they must judge themselves on a regular basis.

So keep reading, and know that you'll learn to love yourself more and more so that the shame others try to put on you can just bounce off your strong core of profound self-regard. The best revenge is becoming so solid in your self-love that the words of others can't penetrate you.

The Freezing Spell

I have had amazing results with this ritual, which helps to neutralize the energy you receive from someone who is unkind or toxic.

1. Write a letter to God, the Universe, or your spirit guides (whatever you prefer), asking them to block the energy coming from this unkind, toxic person. Here's an example: "Dear spirit guides: Please block the energy coming from Diana, and protect me from her negativity. Thank you so much."
2. Find a glass jar, fold the letter, and put it inside the jar. Cover the paper with a small rock, and pour some water over the paper and rock.
3. Place the jar in the freezer, and allow the freezer to freeze all of the negative energy. Leave it there as long as you like. At some point, you may feel that it's safe for you to thaw the water in the jar and discard the paper. If you find that the person begins to unleash negativity on you again, simply repeat the freezing spell.

MINDFUL MOMENT

One day, I was burning up with anger about something so unimportant that I can't even remember what it was. I called a friend and asked her what I should do. She was silent for a moment and then said, "Rather than focus on others and the hurtful things they say, we need to focus on ourselves."

She was so right. You can't control others, but you can control how you react to their negativity. When someone is unkind to me, I imagine that I'm holding a mirror in front of me; I allow their negative comments to reflect back to them. At the same time, I'm reminded that their negativity is a reflection of them, not a reflection of me!

chapter two

IT'S AN INSIDE JOB

I put on the fat suit and went outside and walked around. I was really nervous about being found out, but nobody would even make eye contact with me. It really upset me.
—Gwyneth Paltrow, on her role in the film *Shallow Hal*

I was a normal, well-adjusted kid until I was fourteen. Then my parents divorced, and my world came crashing down around me. So I ran away from home, convinced I "knew everything." I couldn't conceive that there were much worse experiences out there than my family falling apart.

I went to a beach, where I was befriended by a man who listened to me talk about my issues with my parents. He said he had problems with his mom and dad, too. I felt comfortable with him and I trusted him when he asked if I wanted to go and stay at his "friend's" house. I wouldn't know until hours later that the "friend" didn't exist. When I got antsy and said I was going to leave, he offered to walk me back.

Then he attacked me, raping me multiple times over a period of several hours. I wasn't able to escape until morning.

Before the attack, I was completely innocent about the birds and the bees. Nothing about it was even in my vocabulary. I still played with Barbie dolls and had never even kissed a boy. What happened to me was unimaginable. I didn't understand anything about it.

My attacker told me he had watched me for more than an hour, studying me. When I finally escaped him, the grief and shame I felt was overwhelming. What had I done wrong to attract this kind of attention? Why had he chosen *me?*

I felt like I would be "tainted goods" for life. It was the start of deep-seated insecurities that would eventually lead to the binge eating and yo-yo dieting that plagued me for a quarter of a decade.

I ate because a part of me didn't want to be seen. I wasn't consciously aware of it, but deep down, I felt that if I wasn't attractive, I could prevent an attack like that from ever happening to me again. The irony, of course, is that the bigger you are, the more obvious you are. Plus, as we all know, rape is an act of violence, not sex.

But the belief that I'd be safe if I was unattractive was imbedded in me. It helped me to feel as though I had some control over my fate after experiencing something so horrific. So I began to put on weight. Inevitably, I dieted and lost the weight for a while. But as soon as I started to get thin again, I felt unsafe and put the weight back on. And every time I gained weight back, I gained more. If I lost eighty pounds, I gained back a hundred. I went from one extreme to the other, either binge eating or starving myself and exercising like crazy. On both ends of the spectrum, my eating habits were anything but healthy.

It wasn't until I had my surgery and lost the weight that I realized the weight loss wasn't the key to feeling better about myself. I still felt the same on the inside, and none of the pain was gone. The only way to feel better was to change myself on the inside. I had to deal with why I was trying to hide from the world.

It's common for people with weight problems to have trauma in their background. Even people who don't have weight problems have some kind of trauma that causes obstacles to creating what they want in life. No matter what, healing is an "inside job."

If you think your weight issues might have stemmed from trauma, I'm not going to pretend that a book alone will be enough to help you heal. And you can't do it without help. You're going to need an experienced counselor to assist you in getting over the trauma, even if it happened years ago.

That said, this book can be an adjunct to your therapy, or it can help you after you feel that therapy has taken you as far as it can.

For me, the healing process has been a long one, but I'm here to tell you that you *can* recover from terrible, traumatic events. And I know that there are many people who manage to get their stress eating under control. I don't believe it can be done by willpower alone, however. You simply have to go deeper to heal the broken parts within.

As scary as that might seem, it's so worth the effort. I can't imagine what my life would be like today if I hadn't gone deep for my healing journey. With assistance, you can do it, too.

The Five Stages of Grief

You've no doubt heard of the five stages of grief developed by Elisabeth Kübler-Ross, but you probably think of them as what you experience after someone dies. Grief comes in many forms, however, and is not caused only by the death of someone you love. You can grieve anything you lose—your innocence, your formerly thin body, a broken relationship, a job, a house, a way of being, and so on. Whenever you suffer any kind of loss, you go through the stages of grief to some degree. Here they are in order, although bear in mind that you may experience them in a different order or even go back and forth between the stages:

Denial: This first step is disbelief that what you're experiencing really happened. It's a necessary part of the process, especially if the grief is particularly traumatic. This stage is a defense mechanism that helps you cope with the overwhelming feelings so you can calibrate the release of those feelings more slowly. After I was raped, for example, I was in shock, and I was grieving more than just the loss of my innocence. I was also grieving the child I'd been. I was introduced to something adult far beyond my comprehension long before I was emotionally or physically ready for it, so denial was the only way I could keep going.

Anger: When you reach this step, you're starting to feel a little bit stronger—strong enough to at least feel and release the emotion of anger, but perhaps not strong enough yet to experience the vulnerability and pain you feel underneath. Many people fear anger, but it's a natural and healthy emotion whenever you're grieving a loss. It's important to allow your anger, although it's better to try to express it in a way that doesn't hurt others. You can express it in therapy, scream in the shower, write angry letters you never send, or punch a pillow. For a long time, I was very angry at myself and at the world in general.

Bargaining: This stage involves trying to negotiate your pain away. You think *If only this hadn't happened*. In my case, it was *If only I hadn't run away from home and talked to that man, I wouldn't have been raped*. It's a response to the helplessness you feel—the lack of control that causes you to continue to feel unsafe. You might make a pact with God in an effort to feel safer. To a large degree, my overeating was part of the bargaining phase: "If I gain weight, maybe no one will want to rape me again."

Depression: This stage happens when the reality of your loss truly starts to set in, and the day-to-day adjustment to living without what you've lost leaves you in a fog of sadness. Note that this isn't clinical depression, which is due to a chemical imbalance in the brain. This is *situational depression*, and it's a normal part of the grief process. But if you don't move through this step, it can lead to chronic depression. It's important to allow this stage its time, but a therapist can help you move beyond it so that you don't stay stuck in it.

Acceptance: This final phase is when healing truly occurs. You begin to come to terms with what has happened and learn to live without what you've lost. Acceptance doesn't mean you never again feel pain associated with the loss, but you're better able to allow your painful feelings to come to the surface. You also reach a place of coping better with the loss.

Besides the depression stage, you can get stuck in any of the first three stages as well, sometimes for years, if you don't make a concerted effort to move forward. As I look back on my time after the rape, I realize that I got stuck for a long time in the anger phase. People said they felt they had to walk on eggshells around me. I was so upset that my attacker didn't serve prison time for what he'd done to me that I just couldn't move into the next stage. Only through therapy was I able to finally get past the anger. Luckily, the people who loved me cut me a lot of slack during that time and kept me in their lives despite my anger.

As you move through your healing process, stay aware of these stages and recognize that grief is what you're experiencing, even if no one has actually died.

Managing Emotions with Yoga Poses

When intense emotions come to the surface, they can be frightening. You're afraid you're going to be overtaken by them, but that's an unfounded fear. In reality, intense emotions are much more dangerous when they are suppressed. The healthiest thing you can do is allow the feelings to come up and ride their intensity like a wave. I know it isn't fun, but it's better to go through that temporary intensity than to numb out while a volcano is churning below the surface. Living like that can make you physically ill and cause you to feel so numb that you can't even have joyful feelings, all in an effort to keep the painful emotions from making their way to the surface.

I have found that yoga poses help me manage my emotions. If you know yoga, the poses in this chart can help you with the emotions listed on the left. If you aren't familiar with yoga, I highly recommend you try a beginner-level class. Most of these poses can be performed at any level.

Emotion	Yoga Poses
Depression and hopelessness	Child's Pose; Crow Pose; Knees to Chest
Anxiety	Child's Pose; Forward Fold
Lack of self-confidence	Crow Pose; Down Dog; Warrior 2; Fish Pose
Anger and frustration	Eagle Pose; Thread the Needle; Garland Pose
Envy	Mountain Pose; Goddess Pose

Determining Your Negative Beliefs

One of the most powerful aspects of the "inside job" you must do to love yourself and transform your life is to heal your negative beliefs. We develop most of our false, negative beliefs about ourselves and about life very early. Since we're too young to know anything different, we assume these beliefs are facts. But they're actually based either on what we've been taught by the other people in our lives (including other kids) or they're based on our interpretations when we were too young to see the world clearly. Can you think of something you believed as a child that you discovered as an adult was absolutely false? For example, you might have believed that adults are never afraid because the adults around you never showed fear (or never *appeared* to feel fear). As you well know now, that's 100 percent untrue!

Not all beliefs are so easy to disprove, of course, and they must be unearthed from the unconscious before you can become aware of them. This can also be true of the beliefs that are formed later in life, usually because of a traumatic experience. After I was raped at fourteen, I developed the unconscious belief that I could avoid another experience like that if I was heavier. Of course, that was a false belief, but it was comforting to me because it gave me the illusion of some control over something that was utterly terrifying.

Even though most of your beliefs are unconscious, they still affect how you act and react. Until you discover your negative, false beliefs, you can't dismantle them and create new ones. So let's do an exercise to help you begin to discover what beliefs might be holding you back.

Come back to this exercise frequently—perhaps once every couple of months, or even more often. Each time, you'll discover something new that will allow you to go deeper and heal further.

Exercise: Discover Your Beliefs

Write down your answers to the following questions in whatever way you prefer—in a journal or on an electronic device. After each question, I'll give you several examples/possibilities that I hope will spark revelations for you.

1. What do you remember learning from your family about weight or physical appearance?

   Examples:
   - *Overweight people are lazy and have no willpower.*
   - *Overweight people are unattractive.*
   - *Thin people are more worthy of love and more successful in life.*

2. What do you say to yourself about the weight and appearance of others?

   Examples:
   - *Overweight people should wear more flattering clothes.*
   - *That actress has put on some weight. She doesn't look as good.*
   - *I can't believe my heartthrob is going out with someone so painfully thin. A good-looking man would never go for me.*

3. What beliefs do you hold about yourself that prevent you from taking chances?

Examples:
- *I can't start dating until I lose twenty pounds because every guy would just reject me.*
- *My dream job won't be available to me until I'm thinner.*
- *I can't love myself until I have a body I can stand to look at in the mirror.*

4. Once you've written down your beliefs, write down a counterbelief for each.

Example:
- *"I can't love myself until I have a body I can stand to look at in the mirror" becomes "I love myself just as I am."*

At first, you won't buy into your new belief. It will feel strange to you to say it. But I urge you to read the new beliefs every day until the old beliefs feel stranger to you than the new ones.

5. It takes at least twenty-one days to change a pattern, so be sure to read your new beliefs daily for at least three weeks. If it takes you longer to feel stronger about your new beliefs, don't worry. You're not the only one! Just keep at it.

Who Are You, Really?

When you experience trauma, you lose perspective about who you are. It feels like the person you were is gone, and the person who has been through the awful experience is someone new—someone you don't yet know how to be. It's also someone you don't *want* to be. That's certainly the way it was for me after the rape. I didn't want to be *a girl who'd been raped*, and I didn't know how to be that girl. Who I was before that—the innocent child who knew nothing about boys or men—seemed to disappear.

But over the years, I've come to view myself much like the mythical phoenix. I've had to rise up from the ashes and dust myself off multiple times. One of the ways I've learned to do that is by reconnecting with who I am in my essence—the person I am and will always be no matter what trauma I experience.

With that in mind, let's do one more writing exercise to help you get in touch with the true you. This is the you that nothing can touch. It's who you are regardless of what happens to you in life.

Exercise: Who Are You?

1. Make a list of adjectives that you think describe you. My list included: fat, ugly, lazy, and boring.

2. Now, contact your dearest friend and ask if she sees you the way you have described yourself. My best friend assured me that I was none of the words I had written down. In fact, she pointed out specific examples of how I was none of those things.

3. Ask your friend to make a list of adjectives that describe the essence of your being. (Ask someone who is around you a lot so you get adjectives that describe you now. While you're asking for words that describe your essence, I don't want you to have an excuse to dismiss the words you're given because they're said by someone who knew you in the past.) When I did this exercise with my best friend, some of the words that came up

were *amazing*, *beautiful*, *intelligent*, *loving*, *caring*, *giving*, and *attentive*.

4. If you're like me, you might find it difficult at first to see yourself in the way your friend describes. So do this to solidify for yourself that the essence of who you are is the person your friend says you are: Keep the list of words on your wall or somewhere where you'll see them every day. Remind yourself of these adjectives daily until you begin to see yourself through your friend's eyes.

Taking Good Care of #1

Self-care is critical to getting healthier, both physically and emotionally. The more you learn to love yourself, the more you want to take care of your own needs. And the more you take care of your own needs, the more your self-love increases. In turn, the more you love yourself, the more love you have to give others.

In my experience, all of us take better care of our bodies after we've done the inside work of learning to love ourselves more. But I've also discovered that the more we show ourselves love in the actions we take, the more we build on the love we're developing on the inside.

I have found, for example, that many overweight people are codependent. They take care of everyone else rather than themselves. Part of this, again, is from low self-esteem—feeling they won't be loved by others unless they go out of their way to perform for them. If you fall into that category, consider this: If others require you to "do" for them if they will love you, how is that real love? We love people for who they are, don't we?

Many are also so afraid of being called "selfish" that they don't take care of *self* at all. It becomes extreme. Selflessness is a type of martyrdom that simply isn't healthy. In that situation, you put others ahead of yourself, and you end up compensating with food for what you aren't receiving in your life. But food isn't what you really need, so you end up filling yourself with something that can't truly satisfy you. Since you aren't consciously aware of that, however, you unconsciously eat more and more, trying to fill yourself with a poor substitute for the self-love you really crave.

This is why selflessness is so dangerous. Think of it this way: If you allow the gas tank of your car to empty completely, you reduce the life of your engine. You get more miles out of the first half of the tank, and you extend the engine's life if you fill it up before it's empty. Once the tank is empty, of course, the car stops entirely. It has nothing more to give. Have you ever depleted yourself to that degree? Have you ever given so much to other people that you have nothing left? I have! If you pay attention to regular self-care, you can keep filling up your tank before you get to the breaking point.

Bear in mind that if taking care of yourself is new for you, it's almost inevitable that you'll feel guilty the first few times you do it. Expect the guilt, but ignore it! That's just a habitual reaction. Over time, you'll know unequivocally that you deserve to take care of you, and the guilt will stop.

Sometimes, self-care requires saying "no" to taking care of somebody else. (In a later chapter, we'll expand on this by talking about how to set boundaries with others.) The good news is that even small gestures to care for yourself can help you feel like a queen. In other words, even a half hour of time devoted to yourself can be like filling your gas tank all the way up to the top!

Here's a list of some simple things you can do to fill up your tank without breaking the bank:

1. Take a bath. Even a fifteen-minute soak with some sweet-scented bubbles can feel like heaven if you're accustomed to always giving to others.
2. Take a walk in nature or in a museum that you love.
3. Binge-watch your favorite TV show or movie.
4. Tell everyone that you won't be available, and spend quiet time without interruption. Meditate, read, or sleep!
5. If you can afford it, give yourself a night in a hotel or a weekend away either by yourself or with a friend who will honor your desire for self-care. You might even have points on a credit card or elsewhere that you could use for a free hotel stay!
6. Try a new yoga class. Even if you have only enough energy to lie on your yoga mat on your back, a room of people doing yoga provides a healing, spiritual atmosphere.
7. Have a dance party with or without karaoke in your own living room! Yes, all alone, if necessary. Movement can really help propel you forward.
8. Take a long drive. My favorite is to go into the mountains because the twists and turns remind me that there are always going to be twists and turns in life.
9. Treat yourself to something special. Go to an outlet store, and buy a sweet-smelling candle to please your olfactory nerves.
10. Breathe! This one doesn't cost a cent and can lead to many health benefits besides relaxing your spirit. (Try the alternate nostril breathing exercise described in chapter 4.)

Be Your Own First Responder

First responders have the uncanny ability to tune out distracting noise so they can take care of the task at hand. When you find yourself feeling panicky or emotionally distressed, say to yourself, *I'm going to be my own first responder*. See if the "first responder" part of yourself can step outside the panic or emotional distress so you can observe it from a place of calm. Remember: First responders can't panic when they help someone. They have to stay 100 percent focused.

While you serve as your own first responder, you will learn to soothe the part of you that's anxious so you can come to your own aid. It's a wonderful skill to have because it allows you to take care of yourself when no one else may be available to help you.

It will be difficult to do this at first, but keep trying. It's a skill well worth developing; knowing you have it in your back pocket will help you feel much more secure.

MINDFUL MOMENT

When I'm confronted with an obstacle in my life, I think about the hurdles in track-and-field events. In the 100-meter hurdles, competitors run and gracefully glide over the hurdle, run a few more steps, and glide over the next one. So rather than think of the problems in my life as some insurmountable obstacle, I try to view them as just another hurdle that's propelling me closer to the finish line! No matter where you are in your healing process, don't give up. With each hurdle you step over, you're closer to a better life. As someone who has had to jump over many hurdles, I can attest that you'll get there.

chapter three

GETTING THROUGH THE DARK TIMES

Courage doesn't always roar. Sometimes courage is the quiet voice at the end of the day saying, I will try again tomorrow.
—Mary Anne Radmacher

*A*fter being raped at fourteen, I had no real coping mechanisms at first for my trauma and the emotions that came with it. What had happened to me was so inconceivable that I couldn't process it until I got professional help. Eating in an effort to disappear was only one of my problems.

I couldn't bear the thought of going back to my school with the friends who knew what had happened to me. I honestly thought I would rather die than look at people who knew I'd been raped. And so just like that, one day I simply decided I wanted to die. The only way I could think of to end my life was to take some sleeping pills we had around the house. I had no idea how many it would take to kill me, so I just grabbed a few and washed them down.

Shortly after I'd taken them, my brother came into my room. I was startled. It jarred me out of my suicidal stupor, and I flashed for a moment on the reality that he could have found my dead body in my room.

"Do you want me to teach you how to surf in the morning?" he asked cheerfully.

I had been begging him to teach me all summer, and it was what I wanted at that time of my life more than anything. My emotions shifted suddenly. There was something worth living for, something to look forward to. Without knowing it, my brother threw me a lifeline, and just like that, I no longer wanted to die.

I had to stop the pills from killing me. *I need to throw them up*, I thought. I wasn't sure what would work, so I tried drinking an entire pot of coffee. It did the trick, and the pills came up and out into the toilet. I managed to get to sleep, knowing that in the morning, I would get to try surfing.

The next day, I don't even remember waking up, but first thing, I went into my brother's room and woke him up. His promise had saved me.

After that, I didn't feel suicidal again for a long time. But once I reached adulthood and was married, those awful feelings revisited me when I was working in the bakery that my then-husband and I owned together. One of our employees was very thin. She was one of those women who will always be under one hundred pounds, no matter how much she eats. She came up to me one day and asked, "Did you hear your friends over there talking about you?"

"They aren't my friends. Their kids go to the same school as my daughter, but that's it."

"Well, they were talking about how your body mass index is increasing in size every day and that they can't believe you have such a good-looking husband. They wonder what he sees in you."

I couldn't fathom why anyone would tell me such a thing. Was she trying to be cruel?

"Why would you tell me this?" I asked her.

"I thought you should know that they aren't really your friends."

"I already told you they aren't my friends, so I don't see the point in telling me their hurtful comments."

I ducked into the bathroom and began to sob. I would have to face those women every school day, and I'd have to pretend that I didn't know what they said about me. *They only care about my weight. They don't care that I have a good moral compass and a big heart. If I'm making so many people miserable because I'm fat, maybe it would be better if I wasn't here anymore*, I said to myself.

That day, I knew I was going to end my life. I figured out a plan, and I was going to make it happen.

When I got home, I was immediately confronted with the news that our dog, Buddy, was very sick. I knew he hadn't been doing well, but I had no idea he was so close to death. As I sat down and held him, he died quietly in my arms.

My five-year-old daughter came downstairs and asked, "What's the matter with Buddy?" Suddenly, I was forced to explain the concept of death to my young daughter. I looked at Buddy. His pain was over. The pain of those of us left behind was just beginning. And I knew that if I killed myself, my pain would be over quickly. But I'd leave behind so much pain, particularly for my little girl.

The finality of Buddy's death jarred me and pulled me out of myself and my own sadness. I realized I could never put my daughter through that. Even though I was grief-stricken to lose my beloved dog, he gave me a tremendous gift that day. He showed me the pain I would inflict on my child if I killed myself.

Five years later, I was reminded of the same thing. Maybe the universe was just making sure I didn't think about killing myself again. Someone told me that a mutual acquaintance had lost her mother to suicide at age ten. This acquaintance always seemed to walk around with a dark cloud of sadness about her. My daughter was exactly ten years old at the time, so it showed me what her life would probably be like if she were to lose me like that. I couldn't bear the thought of her going through her entire life with a dark cloud around her because her mother had committed suicide.

Now, I'm not suggesting that you pin your entire reason for being on another person. Even if they aren't consciously aware of it, they'll feel the burden of that, and it isn't fair to them. But when that darkness threatens to take over, it can certainly help to think of what your demise would do to the people you love. Suicide leaves them feeling terribly guilty. They wonder if they could have done something to stop you.

Here's the bottom line: when you go through dark times, find something that helps you hold on. After my brother taught me how to surf when I was fourteen, I told him I had planned to kill myself. He was only about a year older than me, but he said something very wise: "Nicole, there's always a pull between life and death inside us. We have to find the strength to fight for another day." He was so right.

At fourteen, what helped me fight for another day was the promise of learning how to surf. It was as simple as the opportunity to try something that sounded pleasurable and was new. Later in life, what helped me fight for another day was wanting to be here for my daughter and not wanting to inflict unnecessary pain on her life.

Of course, I also would have missed out on so much joy and so many wonderful experiences that I've had since the times when I contemplated killing myself. *Things do get better.*

What do you do when you find yourself in a dark place, whatever the reason? The best way I know how to fight for another day is to find a good reason to keep going—a reason for being (preferably something other than food, of course). Or maybe just remind yourself of this story: Every year, people jump off the Golden Gate Bridge in San Francisco. Few survive it, but a handful do. Interviews with those people prove that almost all of them regretted jumping the moment their hands let go of the bridge. As they fell toward the water of the bay, they wished they hadn't jumped. They knew there were reasons to stay, people who could love them, and pleasures to be experienced.

What about you? Let's explore what might bring you pleasure in those moments when you need it most.[1] Some of the items on the self-care list in the last chapter might be a good place to start!

---

[1] Obviously, I'm not trying to trivialize suicidal feelings or clinical depression. If you have a chemical imbalance or other mental illness that prevents you from deriving joy from anything in your life, please get professional help. You're one of a kind, and the world really does need you!

Exercise: Pleasure Lists

This exercise is in three parts. You'll write two short lists and then write a short letter to yourself.

Part 1: First, write down what brings you pleasure or joy. I know it can sometimes be difficult to think of anything, especially if you're sad or depressed. But so often, we take for granted the small things that can bring us a lot of pleasure if we just open our hearts to them. For example, one of my friends loves birds, so she makes a point of noticing them when she walks around her city. She looks at their delicate feathers and connects with their innate sweetness.

It's a cliché, but taking time to smell the roses really can work. Notice flowers, plants, children, and animals—the innocent things around you. Go to an art museum if you appreciate art. Do everything you can to find something to be grateful for in your world. If you take pleasure in freshly washed sheets, wash them! Maybe add a scent that you love. Engage your senses as much as you can. Wrap yourself in the softest fabric you own, and really feel it against your skin. Enjoy the simple things as much as possible.

If you have kids, plan a craft project with them. If you don't have kids, maybe you know someone who does. You could plan a play date with them and enjoy their company. No one will show you how to experience joy in the small things better than a young child.

If you live near a body of water and like water, take yourself there if you can. Watch the flow of the water. If there's a tide, notice the ebb and flow and recognize that your life also has ebbs and flows. Even if you're experiencing an ebb right now, there will come a time when you'll have flow again.

Give yourself a spa treatment either at an actual spa or at home. Maybe you have a friend who would give you a facial if you reciprocate.

Now that I've given you some ideas, make a list of everything you can think of that brings you pleasure and joy. Then, on one of those days when you're sinking down into the darkness, pull out your list, and make sure you experience one or two of the things you love.

Part 2: Next, think about what you've looked forward to in your life that you haven't yet experienced—like my desire to learn how to surf. Have you always wanted to learn to knit? Get some yarn and pull up a YouTube video tutorial. Is there a botanic garden in your area that you've always wanted to visit? Make a plan to finally go. Maybe take pictures when you're there. Have you always wanted to visit Paris? Maybe you can't hop on a plane and go there, but you could still let yourself dream. You could plan the trip as if you were going (guarding against feeling down because you can't actually go!). Download Google Earth on your computer, and take a stroll around the city's streets. Think about where you would go and what you'd do. Imagine yourself there. Then, if it's a possibility, start to put money away toward actually going! (I will show you a way to start this vacation fund in chapter 5.)

Now, make your list of the things you've always wanted to do—both what you might actually be able to do and what you think you might never be able to do. The truth is that just by writing it down, you're putting the universe on notice that you want it, and you just might be surprised someday in the future that your wish has come true. It has happened to me more than once—and it's happened to lots of people I know!

Keep both of your lists in a handy place so that you can access them when you need them.

Part 3: Lastly, pretend that you're the friend of someone who's feeling just like you. This friend tells you she no longer sees any reason for living. She doesn't think she has anything to live for or anything to offer anyone else. She thinks the world would be better off without her. Or maybe she just thinks she's ugly or unworthy. Write a letter to this friend. What would you say to this person? Be your best friend. You know how. I know you do! Here's the letter I wrote to myself. Feel free to use it as a guide.

> *Dear Nicole,*
> *I see how much pain you are in, and I want you to know that your pain is real and that I will never discount that. What I also want you to see is how much of an impact you have made on the people around you. I know you think that the world doesn't need you in it anymore, but I'm telling you that you're wrong. What the world needs more of is people exactly like you—people who are passionate and kind. Compassion for others is one of your greatest gifts. I have seen people's faces light up just at the sight of you. There is always a struggle between life and death. That's never going to go away. But if you can focus just on this second and stay present, you will get through this. You have conquered far too many*

obstacles to give up now. Look at your calendar right now, Nicole, and find something that you're looking forward to. If you can't do it right away, plan it. You have always had the power over your own destiny, and believe me when I tell you how much I love you. This is not how your story ends. Not by a long shot. So please, find an event to look forward to, and call your friends. Tell them you're sad (you don't have to get into specifics), and let them know you're looking forward to seeing them. They will respond and will have your back.

Love,
Your Best Friend

Meditation: Finding Light in the Darkness

The ancient poet Hafiz once wrote, "I wish I could show you, when you are lonely or in darkness, the astonishing light of your own being." When we're going through difficult times, it can be very hard to see any light in the darkness. This meditation is designed to help you find that small point of light and expand on it like we did in chapter 1, allowing it to grow and eventually overtake the darkness.

1. Sit in a comfortable chair with your feet planted firmly on the ground. Rest your arms at your sides, on top of your thighs or on the arms of the chair.

2. Close your eyes, and feel the earth beneath your feet. Feel how it supports you. No matter what else is happening in your life, you automatically have the support of the earth. Imagine that there's a string extending from your spine down into the earth, keeping you grounded and safe.

3. Now, imagine another string is extending from the top of your head all the way to the top of the sky. This is your connection to the sky and to spirit, offering you even more safety.

4. Tune into yourself and the easy rhythm of your breathing, and imagine that there's a point of white light somewhere in your body. Allow it to appear wherever it wants. If it doesn't appear, willfully place it wherever you like. The light may be extremely bright or faint. It may be small or large. This is the light of possibility, hope, and a positive future.

5. Notice as you breathe that you can expand and contract the light with your breath. As you inhale, make the light become wider. As you exhale, see the light contract a bit. Breathe in and out five times as you watch the light get bigger and smaller.

6. Now that you realize you have some control over this light, see if you can make it grow. Willfully make the light bigger until it takes up more space in your mind's eye. Continue to add to the light, making it progressively bigger. How big can you make it? Can you make it so big that there's no darkness at all anymore? Make your light as big as you can, maybe even so big that this light of possibility, hope, and a positive future is all there is—inside you and all around you. Linger in that light as long as you want. You can even let yourself fall asleep if you like.

7. When you're ready, begin to come back from your meditative state by wiggling your fingers and toes.

Gently let your head roll from side to side. Open your eyes slowly and look around until you feel fully awake.

8. Keep the image of your bright light in your mind. Whenever you start to feel dark again, inhale and exhale five times, seeing the light in your mind's eye, and allow it to expand and bring you comfort.

Find a Purpose

When we have a purpose—a reason for being—we stop focusing as much on our own pain. Instead, we focus on what we can do to make the world a more joyful, beautiful, or loving place.

Believe me, I know all too well that when you feel like a worthless person, you're convinced that you don't have anything to offer others. But often, all it takes to help someone else is a moment of our attention, a simple smile, or a helping hand. Have you ever experienced something simple like that from someone and had it turn your mood around? Maybe a stranger wished you a beautiful day with complete sincerity or held the door open for you.

You can give yourself a sense of purpose as simply as that—by just smiling at a stranger, holding the door open for someone, or telling the cashier at the gas station that you hope he has a beautiful night. Even if the person isn't friendly, *you* can be friendly. Maybe that individual is feeling much like you do, as though life has nothing to offer him and he has nothing to offer anyone else. You may never know it, but that simple gesture could give him the tiny ray of light he needs to make it through to the next day. So even if you're an introvert, force yourself to say, "Have a good night" to the cashier at the grocery store. Even if it's the last thing you feel like doing. It will help to pull you out of your own pain.

If it's possible for your schedule and circumstances, look into ways to do volunteer work. Anything that will take you out of yourself is good for you! Remember the self-care discussion in the last chapter, however, and don't give to the point of depleting yourself. But if you can find a way to focus on how you can serve others and make their lives better rather than worry about whether they like you, even if it's in the tiniest of ways, it can make a big difference in how you feel.

Without realizing it, you may diminish the role you already play in others' lives every day. Let's say you deliver packages, and you think of it as an unimportant job. But maybe you're delivering vital medicine to a heart patient or a new dress to a teenager who's excited to go to her prom. These people rely on you. Remember that you're part of the bigger scheme of things in this world!

By putting your focus on the contribution you already make or *can* make to others, you'll gain perspective on your own situation.

Here are some other ideas: You could call a nursing home and ask if you could stop by and visit residents or drop off a handmade card or drawings by your kids to give to the residents. (Note that they probably won't allow you to bring food or live flowers.) Maybe you have an elderly neighbor who could use a lift to the grocery store or the doctor. Actively look for ways you can help others in a way that feels good to you (and not as a way to get them to like you), and you'll no longer feel that the world would be better off without you.

But truly, all you need to think about is leaving the people you encounter during your day feeling better than they did before. Again, all it takes is a smile or a kind word. If you're shy, a quiet but sincere "Have a great day" can be enough. Don't ever discount how much these small kindnesses can mean to others!

Exercise: Purpose Plan

This time, I'll ask you to make a list of what you can do to serve others. Think of small ways each day, and/or make a bigger plan to visit a nursing home, visit the children's ward of a hospital, help out a neighbor, or become a volunteer for a nonprofit. I've already given you lots of ideas. What will you do to spread love in your part of the world? Remember that you can keep it simple!

My Own Sense of Purpose

I got a big lesson about purpose when my husband and I were going through our divorce. He wanted to buy me out of my share of our bakery business so that he could run it himself. But I had spent a decade using that bakery as my sole source of income. I'd put my heart and soul into it, so I was reluctant to just hand it over to him. Plus, what would I do for money?

That's when my divorce attorney gave me a reality check. "You can stay partners with him in the restaurant, but in my experience, this never goes well. It might work for a year or two, but eventually, you'll have a disagreement. It'll all fall apart. You're better off just co-parenting with him, not also owning a business with him. My advice is to find your real purpose, and let him have the bakery."

It took me a month to process that conversation. I couldn't wrap my mind around giving him the business we had built together. But it wasn't like running a bakery had ever been my life's ambition. Sure, I enjoyed parts of it, but the truth was that owning that bakery had contributed to my suicidal feelings. People there constantly talked about my weight. They'd go on review websites and complain that I was too fat, as if my pounds somehow ruined the taste of their pastry. When I had worked previously as a massage therapist in a spa, I never got comments like that.

Eventually, I realized that it was illogical and destructive to be unwilling to give up a business that had been my personal nemesis. I was holding on to something negative like a security blanket. When I was confronted with this realization, I broke down in tears. What I really wanted to do was be a writer like my father. Maybe I could make a living at it; maybe not. But I could find another way to make a living and write in my free time. I didn't have to make my income in a business that was painful. Life's too short!

Maybe you don't know what you want to be "when you grow up," but at the very least, begin to think about it. What could be your purpose in life? What have you always wanted to do? Even if you can't make a living at it, start to make time for it in your life. If you want to write, take some time to write. Don't worry whether your writing is good. Just write for yourself. If you want to paint, paint. Again, don't worry if it's good. You don't have to show it to anyone. If you want to work with kids, find a way to move toward that goal, even if it's just as a volunteer. Look for what gives you pleasure in your life, and it will start to matter less and less what you weigh or what other people think about you. It will start to feel like you have a reason for being.

But whatever you do, please hear this: The mold was broken when you were born, and even if you can't see it, there is no one else on earth who can take your place. You have a reason for being here, and you deserve your corner of the universe. No one else has a right to rob you of knowing that. I know that just by virtue of the fact that you're reading this book, you have a good heart. We *need* all the people we can get with good hearts. Let your heart be seen, and you'll realize how much you deserve.

Someone Always Has It Worse

I would never try to diminish your pain or tell you that you don't have a right to feel your feelings. Trust me—I would *never* do that!

At the same time, when you're feeling like you don't want to go on, it can help to get some perspective: There's always someone who has it worse, and sometimes, that can give you the strength to fight for another day, like my brother said.

A few years ago, my friend went to a screening of a documentary about the West Memphis Three—three teenagers who were falsely accused of murdering a couple of boys in West Memphis, Arkansas. They were in prison for many years. One of them was even held in solitary confinement for a crazy amount of time with no sunlight. To this day—he is now in his forties—he has to wear dark glasses indoors because his eyes were damaged from the lack of light in his cell.

The three men had been released just three weeks before the screening, and they agreed to be in the documentary to talk about what they endured. A couple of years later, my friend had occasion to meet Damien Echols, the one who had been in solitary confinement. She couldn't believe how sweet and friendly he was. In fact, the "lightness" of his energy made her cry after she walked away from him. She was amazed that he could come out of such an experience with love in his heart.

For a while after encountering the West Memphis Three, my friend had a sign on her wall in front of her computer that read, "You're not one of the West Memphis Three." It was a reminder to her that even if her life became horribly challenging, it still wasn't as bad as what those three guys endured. It gave her perspective and helped her get through some tough times. If they could keep going and come out of prison as loving people, she could keep going, too.

MINDFUL MOMENT

While writing this chapter, I got word that the mother of a close friend had lost her battle with cancer. It reminded me how important it is to wake up each day with gratitude. There are many people who aren't given the option to live; getting old is a privilege denied to many, as they say. When we hear about others passing away, we can take a much-needed step back and be thankful that we're still here and can find our true purpose! We have an opportunity, no matter how much we weigh, to make a difference in the world.

chapter four

BODY ARMOR AND BOUNDARIES

No is a complete sentence.
—Anne Lamott

As is often the case for the victim of any kind of assault, trying to prosecute my rapist caused additional and continuous trauma for me. When the police found him, he asked, "Are you picking me up for what I did to that little girl?" Yet even with his ready confession, there were people who didn't believe I was telling the truth.

I made a few key mistakes when I returned home the morning after the rape that would forever alter the outcome of the case. I was exhausted, and even using a scrub brush wouldn't have stopped me from feeling dirty. But I showered before I told anyone, washing away the evidence. Because of that, the district attorney felt the case wasn't strong enough to get a conviction. I was young and naïve and believed if I could just tell my story in court, I would be believed. But the DA said I was too emotional to make a good witness.

Sure enough, when we went before a judge to determine if a trial would be held, the judge ruled that there wasn't enough evidence to pursue a criminal case. My rapist walked right out the door of the courthouse that same day. As you can imagine, I was devastated and terrified. Would he look for me and try to hurt me for telling? Would this ever be over?

As luck would have it, however, my rapist left a pair of shoes at the jail. Just before he called to ask if he could pick them up, a fax arrived at the police station from another state. My rapist was wanted in another state for armed robbery, aggravated assault, and attempted murder.

"Sure, come and pick up your shoes," a police officer told him. As soon as he walked in the door, they handcuffed him. Since he was going by a false name in California and committed perjury when he testified under that name, he served time in my state before he was extradited to the other state. *But he never served any time for what he did to me. There was never any justice for the crime against me.*

To this day, I have no idea what happened to the man. I didn't follow his case, nor do I remember his name.

While knowing he was in custody helped me feel a little bit safer, there's no question that the entire experience—from the rape to the court hearing to the lack of justice and closure—took an enormous toll on me. It's no wonder that so many rape victims never tell anyone. I'm not sorry that I told; it would have been worse for me if I hadn't. But the experience of telling law enforcement and being subjected to court procedures is also traumatic. Anyone who goes through that needs support!

In my case, I don't think anyone understood what I truly needed. As an adolescent, I certainly didn't know what to ask for.

So it's no surprise that I had my first nervous breakdown about three weeks after the rape. I looked in a mirror one day and saw myself as a broken, fragmented, and worthless "thing." I didn't even see myself as a human being. I hated myself that much. *How could I let this happen to me?* I thought. In my mind, it was all my fault.

I started banging my head against the mirror. Then I slammed the door against my forehead. I think I wanted to change my appearance in some way because I couldn't stand the sight of myself. I probably would have continued until I knocked myself out if my brother hadn't come to my rescue once again. He wrapped his arms around me and bear-hugged me until I calmed down. About a week later, I was admitted to a mental hospital. I spent two years there while they treated me for severe depression and suicidal ideation.

When I came out of the hospital, I was a stronger person, but it took me a long time to get over the shame that I felt because I'd been raped. I now know there's no shame in something like that, but it was a long journey to get to that place. I also had a lot of shame around having spent two years in a mental hospital. I feared that everyone in the world would just see me as "crazy." The truth is that my parents were trying to keep me safe, mostly from myself. Throughout my life, I'm the person who has most stood in my own way.

Even with the help of the therapists at the hospital, I developed my own coping mechanisms in order to feel safe enough to keep living in the world. Body armor became one of my primary ones.

Food became the friend that never let me down. Today, I lovingly refer to that extra weight as "my shield." It kept me sane for a long time because, as I've already told you, I believed that if I was unattractive, no one would rape me again. Even though it was a false assumption, putting on weight helped me feel like I could keep going.

Can you relate? Using weight to shield one's self from others is a common problem. I recently met a woman who admitted to me that she had just lost eighty pounds and had been a yo-yo dieter her whole life. Since I'm slim—and it's been years since my weight-loss surgery—she assumed I'd never had a weight problem. She also assumed I couldn't possibly understand what she was going through. In other words, she inadvertently fit-shamed me!

"Stop right there," I told her. "You don't know the struggles I've been through. I lost one hundred pounds five years ago after yo-yo dieting most of my life. In fact, I'm writing a book about it, and I've come to realize that the reason I put on the weight was trauma."

With that, she started to cry. "That's my story, too."

"It's everyone's story," I said to her gently.

You may have heard Oprah talk about this same thing. We armor ourselves with added weight as we console ourselves with food. And as we armor ourselves, we shut people out to a large degree both physically and emotionally in order to try to avoid being hurt again. It isn't logical, but it's a common response to being hurt.

The problem is that as the armor seems to protect us from others, it also isolates us from them and creates a perpetual state of loneliness. Even if we're constantly surrounded by people, we don't let them in. We don't let them see who we really are. We might feel vulnerable to the point of feeling downright raw, but we don't allow ourselves to be vulnerable with anyone from a place of choice and empowerment. You see, there's a lot of power in choosing to be vulnerable as opposed to feeling vulnerable out of fear and having no control.

Body armor causes you to live half a life. Not only are you bogged down with weight that diminishes your physical health, but you're unhappy about how you look. Often, you're even restricted as to what you can do. Maybe you can't play with your kids, go out dancing, or go on hikes with friends. Emotionally, it prevents you from having the deep relationships with others that you long for the most—the kinds of relationships that make life worth living.

So how do you begin to break free from that armor when it's such a habit to protect yourself like that?

Determining Safety

Like all the work involved in healing, breaking free of your body armor isn't easy. You might need therapy to do it, and it could take you a good while to heal the trauma and fear at the root of it. But the time to start that healing is now, because your life will improve at least to some degree the minute you take action to get better. You might have to deal with some intense feelings in the process, but remember: Those feelings involve *temporary* pain, while the numbness and unwillingness to heal involve *lifelong* pain.

You might find that as you heal the internal, emotional armor, your physical weight begins to drop automatically; that's what happens to many. In my case, as you've already learned, I needed to undergo surgery. Whatever you need for you is perfectly fine.

But as you're healing your body armor, losing the weight (or not), and allowing yourself to be more vulnerable with others—one pound at a time and one step at a time—you'll need a way to determine who is safe and who isn't. How can you figure out whether someone is worthy of your empowered vulnerability?

If you've been seriously harmed, it can be scary to open yourself up to anyone. In truth, dealing with any person involves some degree of risk. There's no guarantee you won't be hurt again. But the stronger you can become inside, the more resilient you'll be and the better able you'll be to withstand whatever hurt comes your way. After all, not everyone will attack you. Most people are just flawed human beings like all the rest of us—people who make mistakes and sometimes hurt others when they don't mean to.

Of course, I can't provide you any foolproof way to determine if someone is safe. I can't guarantee you that it's okay to let down your emotional armor in any given situation. But I do think there are ways you can feel more confident about it. And the best way I know to do that is to get in touch with your intuition, so let's talk about that next.

The Wisdom of Intuition

When I was overweight, I often tried to talk myself out of going to parties. I felt everyone would judge me for my weight, and I was sure I'd feel uncomfortable. In one instance, I chose not to go to an event because it was on the beach, and I just couldn't see myself there in a swimsuit around everyone else. One of the women who would be there was very ill with cancer. My gut—my intuition—told me very clearly that if I didn't go, I'd miss an important opportunity to see her. But I couldn't get past my worries of being judged, so I chose to ignore my intuitive feelings.

As it turned out, this friend passed away very shortly after the beach party, and since I didn't go, I never had the chance to say goodbye to her. It's something I'll always regret.

Another time, the voice of fear inside me told me once again not to go to a party because I'd probably be judged and disliked due to my weight. But my intuition told me to go. "You just might have a good time," it said.

In that particular instance, I listened to my gut and went to the party. I met so many wonderful women that night, and not one of them disliked me. They all thought I was engaging, charming, and funny—all the things I am no matter how much I weigh. And every single one of those women has stayed a friend or at least a close acquaintance since then. I hate to think of what I would have missed if I had ignored my intuition that night.

When you have food issues, staying in touch with your intuition is especially complicated. If you're in touch with it, you can't eat beyond what satisfies your actual hunger. You have to tune out that intuitive voice in order to keep overeating. This can make it harder for you to trust yourself in other aspects of your life.

The other issue is that when you experience trauma, you disconnect from your intuition. You lose trust in your ability to determine when you're safe and when you're not. To heal and begin to gradually let down your armor, you must find a way to reconnect with your intuition. In my experience, the body is the quickest doorway in. It's the gut feeling that you've probably had at least once in your life. If you can begin to cultivate your ability to connect with your gut, you'll reduce your risk of getting hurt by others.

When making decisions, having a clear sense of your intuition or your gut is so important. Your mind can too easily overanalyze a situation, while your heart may tell you what you want to hear. For example, your heart will tell you that you won't gain weight if you eat that extra piece of cake or that it's okay because you'll start your diet tomorrow.

Your intuition, on the other hand, gives you a signal regarding whether something is a good idea or a bad idea. It tells you whether someone is trustworthy. While I may not read its signals accurately 100 percent of the time, I've found that my odds of making good decisions are much better when I check in with my intuition.

But how can you tell that your intuition is speaking rather than your mind or heart? I'm not going to pretend it's easy, but you can develop the ability to tune in to it. I get a strange feeling in my shoulder, for example, if I sense something is "off" about someone I've met. Have you ever had an experience like that? Let's explore ways to turn down the volume on your mind and turn up the volume of your body.

Finding Your Intuition

I truly believe we are all intuitive beings, but we aren't taught to use that ability in our culture. Here is a list of some of the best ways to reconnect with your intuition.

1. **Meditation:** When you meditate, you allow the rational mind to rest, and you get in touch with the intuitive mind. If you aren't accustomed to meditating, it can be hard at first to quiet your mind. This is why I suggest starting small with perhaps one minute of meditation in the morning and one minute in the evening. When one minute starts to feel too short, add another minute or two, gradually increasing the time you meditate.

2. **Pay attention to how you feel:** When you're in the presence of another person, what's the first thing that comes to mind? How do you feel in your body? Do you feel at ease or nervous? Of course, you might feel nervous because you admire the person and feel inferior to her. But it could be that you feel nervous because you don't feel safe. If you're like most other people, you probably don't bother to ask yourself these kinds of questions. If you make it a practice to ask yourself how you feel, you'll begin to notice your intuition in relation to the people in your life. You'll become more aware of why you don't feel comfortable. One thing is

for sure, though: If it feels bad to be with someone, it probably *is* bad.

3. **Use all five senses:** Intuition is the sixth sense, but to get in touch with it, you need to connect better with the other five senses: sight, hearing, taste, touch, and smell. If you notice your five senses more intently, you'll also begin to feel your sixth sense more easily.

4. **Don't discount your intuition:** Many times, you feel or sense something "off" about a person or situation, but you discount that sense and talk yourself out of paying attention to it. When you ignore your intuition, you're much more likely to get into trouble. Trust your gut!

Using Your Body as a Pendulum

Here's another way to test your intuition. It might seem too far out for you, but I invite you to give it a try.

First, relax and feel your feet firmly planted on the ground. Take a few deep breaths, and make sure the exhale is about as long as the inhale. When you feel connected to the earth, close your eyes.

Stand straight while you ask yourself a "yes" or "no" question. Then, wait to see if your body begins to tilt forward or backward. If it tilts forward, you've received a "yes." If it tilts backward, you've received a "no." If your body doesn't tilt either way, the answer is neutral.

The Importance of Boundaries

It's vital that you learn to soften your armor and allow people in, but it's also important that you learn to set boundaries, especially with the people your intuition indicates aren't good for you. It takes some major "adulting" to do this, but it's a big part of the job of growing up. And I'm living proof that it can be done!

What are boundaries? Wikipedia defines them as "personal guidelines, rules, or limits that a person creates to identify reasonable, safe, and permissible ways for other people to behave toward them and how they will respond when someone passes those limits." Boundaries are how you prevent yourself from being used and manipulated by others.

In the past, my boundaries weren't strong, and I often let people walk all over me. That kind of behavior is a symptom of the codependency we've already discussed. Here's a fairly common, innocuous example. Right after my daughter was born, we visited my husband's family in France, but he wasn't with us at the time. His family knew I loved *epoisse*, a French cheese, so they fed it to me every single meal for two weeks straight. I can't even be near that cheese anymore. If I had spoken up and taken care of myself, I'd probably still have a love affair with the cheese.

How silly was that? They weren't trying to step over my boundaries. They were simply trying to be good hosts. They probably wouldn't have been offended if I had simply declined the cheese after I'd had my fill. Even with my limited French, I'm sure I could have conveyed that I'd like to skip it for a few days and have some more soon while expressing my appreciation for their kindness in getting me a food they knew I loved.

So many of my stories seem to involve food, so here's another example that isn't quite so innocuous: After my divorce, I briefly dated someone who worked in the culinary field. Even though I've never liked meat and have been a vegetarian my whole life, he was determined that I was going to learn to like meat.

Rather than put my foot down and say I didn't want to eat meat, I disappointed myself and ate it anyway—just to please him. That night, I became violently ill. It was such a great lesson about boundaries for me. I was so focused on taking care of him that I didn't take care of myself, resulting in actual physical illness.

Finally, I stood up to him and said, "Look, I'm a vegetarian, and I don't want to eat meat. And I don't want anyone trying to convince me to eat it." Once I was direct about my boundaries, he apologized.

We aren't taught boundaries in school, and most families have few, if any. As a result, most of us try to make sure everyone is pleased, while displeasing ourselves in the process. It can be so insidious that we have no idea we're doing it. We're so accustomed to it that it feels normal . . . but it isn't.

For example, a friend of mine finally began to notice how she nearly always deferred to the wishes of others rather than honor her own. It happened with friends while choosing restaurants and movies. Her own desires and preferences were unimportant to her, as long as her friends were happy.

Of course, it happens in ways much more serious than just what movie or cuisine you'll enjoy some night. For example, someone might allow a parent to dictate what they do into adulthood or a spouse to control what they do and who they see.

There's nothing wrong with compromise or generosity, but why should your own wants always take a backseat to everyone else's? It's a self-betrayal that's borne of low self-esteem. You don't believe you'll be loved unless you make sure others get what they want—your own wants be damned.

How do you know if you're allowing your boundaries to be annihilated? You may simply need to start paying attention in your life day to day. Are you getting what you want in most situations, or are you always deferring to someone else? You can also use your intuition skills. If you tune in to your body, how do you feel about the situation? Are you uncomfortable, unhappy, or even angry? If you feel victimized or resentful, it's a pretty sure sign that you're allowing your boundaries to be violated.

If so, what would help you to feel differently? What would have to change for you to feel that your boundaries were no longer being violated?

Standing up for myself with the man I was dating was difficult for me, but it was important that I love myself enough to do that. It's true that when someone is accustomed to walking all over your boundaries, it may be hard for them to adjust to a new way of being. In fact, some people won't be able to make that adjustment. If that's the case, you have to ask yourself what's more important—taking care of yourself or taking care of someone else?

In some instances when the other person refuses to honor your boundaries, you may decide to let the relationship go. In other instances, you won't want to do that. For example, if it's your parent, you may decide to deal with the issue the best you can, asserting your needs when possible and deferring to keep the peace when necessary. But if you do it from a place of conscious choice and empowerment rather than fear and victimhood, it will make a huge difference. Only you can decide how to handle each individual circumstance in your life. I just urge you not to give up too easily on setting your boundaries. Treat yourself with respect!

When you first begin to set boundaries with the people in your life, you'll probably feel scared. They might become angry. They might walk away from you. I'm not going to lie to you—those risks are real. But the alternative is to treat yourself like a second-class person—like someone who doesn't deserve what you truly deserve. It also puts you in a position of having unhealthy and unsatisfying relationships.

I suggest starting small and rehearsing what you're going to say. Be direct, but try not to be too accusatory. Talk more about how *you* feel than what the other person did. For example: "When you insist that I eat meat, I feel uncomfortable. I'm a vegetarian, and I don't want to eat meat. Period. I'd appreciate it if you'd honor how I feel about that and stop trying to get me to eat it."

Here's another example: "Mom, I know you have my best interests at heart, but it's my life, and I've decided I'm not going to medical school. I don't want to be a doctor, and I'd appreciate it if you'd honor the decision I've made for my life."

Of course, if Mom objects, you can continue to assert your will rather than getting into an argument: "I hear you, but I've made my decision. And it's my choice to make—no one else's."

If Mom *still* refuses to let it go, you might say, "My decision is final, and I won't entertain any further discussion about this. If you insist on trying to impose your opinion on me about this, I won't be able to talk to you again until you stop."

As you can see, it's important that you stay firm, but it's also helpful if you can keep emotion out of it as much as possible. This can be very difficult, of course, especially if you have pent-up anger toward someone who has been stepping on your boundaries for years or even decades.

If that's the case, I recommend getting the anger out as much as you can *before* you confront the person in question. Scream into a pillow or beat a pillow with your fists. You could also write a letter to the person but not deliver the letter. Allow yourself to say anything you want in the letter. Let all of your anger out. Keep this letter well hidden, of course, so it isn't found. After you've gotten the emotion out, it's a good idea to shred or burn the letter. If it's on your computer, delete it.

The most important thing, however, is that you practice asserting yourself. I can't tell you what a difference it will make in your life. Your self-esteem will skyrocket as you treat yourself with the caring that you deserve. You'll become your own best advocate—again, your own first responder. You'll be your own rescuer!

Create Your Own Hard-No Box

A *Hard No* is something that you absolutely cannot and will not tolerate. Let's make a list of yours and perhaps put them in a box.

1. Decide if you want to have a physical box for your list of Hard Nos, or if you'll write them down and destroy the list, simply storing them from then on in your mind. This is important: if you have a physical box and you don't want anyone else to see what's inside it, you need to think about how you will protect your privacy.
2. Think about what you absolutely would not tolerate. List each one. These are the main things that go against your core values. Here are some examples: I won't tolerate anyone telling me what to eat or not eat. I won't tolerate mean comments about me.
3. Once you know exactly what a Hard No is for you, try to find the place in your physical body where you feel the "no" loud and clear. This area of your body can be a place to check your intuition. When you aren't sure whether to say "yes" or "no," check in with this part of your body. Is it a "no"?
4. If you decide to keep a physical box, add to your Hard-No Box as you think of other things that you won't tolerate.
5. Vow to yourself that you won't violate your Hard Nos. You won't step over your own boundaries in that way, and you won't allow anyone else to do so.
6. Note that your Hard-No list might sometimes change.
7. Trust yourself always. You know deep down what's right for you.

Exercise: Setting Boundaries

In this exercise, you'll begin to determine where in your life you need to set new boundaries.

1. Look at your *Hard-No* list and ask yourself: Who in my life is currently infringing on these boundaries? Choose one person, and write a letter to that person. Let all of your feelings out. Get as angry as you like. Keep writing until all of your feelings have been expressed. If you worry that anyone else could find the letter, destroy it.

2. Next, write down what you might *actually* say to this person in order to assert your new boundary.

3. Repeat steps 2 and 3 for another person (or more) if you wish. You might have boundaries that aren't part of your *Hard-No* list but are *Softer Nos*—things that you *could* tolerate but would rather not. Make note of those, too.

4. If possible, make a plan to speak to some of these people and tell them that you can no longer accept their behavior. It might be as simple as saying "no" the next time they ask something of you that you no longer wish to do. It can be difficult, but you owe it to yourself to stand your ground.

5. If you need to have a conversation with someone about your boundaries, plan ahead so that you can be as loving and calm as possible while also standing firm in your convictions to honor your own boundaries. If you have a good friend who will help you, practice ahead of time using your friend as a sounding board.

What If You're the One Stepping on Someone Else's Boundaries?

There's a good chance that you're also violating someone else's boundaries without realizing it. Don't worry; that's part of being human. But it's a good idea to pay attention to situations in life where you might be inadvertently taking advantage of someone else. For example, do you expect a friend to always listen to your problems without reciprocating?

Become more mindful and self-aware by watching yourself in your life from an observer point of view. Don't judge yourself too harshly. Instead, try to watch like an anthropologist with a healthy curiosity.

If you discover that you've stepped on someone's boundaries, apologize and make amends. Or maybe just quietly change your behavior to be more considerate.

MINDFUL MOMENT

I used to keep old text messages and emails from people who were unkind or had bullied me. One day, I finally woke up and deleted all of those messages. Then I took it a step further and blocked their phone numbers. The moment I couldn't go back and replay those old messages, I felt free. It was a way of setting a boundary with myself. I would no longer allow myself to dwell on negativity. What purpose was served by keeping those messages? Getting rid of the messages and blocking the possibility of future contact was an act of self-love and a declaration that I would no longer tolerate someone who put me down.

chapter five

HEALING BODY DYSMORPHIA

You're damned if you're too thin, and you're damned if you're too heavy. According to the press, I've been both. It's impossible to satisfy everyone, and I suggest we stop trying.
—Jennifer Aniston

When I was fat, I didn't have severe body dysmorphia. I knew I was fat, so I avoided mirrors and didn't scrutinize my body. I already knew I wouldn't like what I saw. I weighed 225 pounds, and I hated it all.

But one day, when the weight was starting to come off and I began to feel better about myself, I made the mistake of looking at my reflection in a store window. I was horrified. Just when I'd started to feel good about wearing a size eight again, the reflection wasn't at all how I thought I looked.

I immediately called a friend and told her what happened. She laughed. "When I look at myself in the reflection of a building window, I feel large and frumpy, too." This was a tall, naturally thin woman! Suddenly, I had some perspective.

But that sense of perspective was short-lived. Body dysmorphia is a tough nut to crack. In my mind, I had an image of the ideal body, perfectly symmetrical without a flaw in sight. And I didn't have that body.

When the dysmorphia really hit me hard was after my weight-loss surgery. I began to look at myself more closely in the mirror, and my hyper-vigilant inner critic came out to play. I was terrified the weight would come back, so my inner critic was quick to tell me that while my body was no longer capable of eating more than one bite of birthday cake, I didn't deserve to eat even that one bite.

My doctor finally calmed my irrational fears four years after my surgery. Gently placing her hand on my shoulder, she said, "Relax. The weight won't come back. You're past the danger zone. But you need to deal with your body dysmorphia because that's a bigger issue than worrying about gaining a pound here or there."

"How can you tell I have body dysmorphia?" I asked her.

She responded with such kindness, and it felt wonderful to be treated so tenderly. But it also made me painfully aware of how unkind I'd been to myself for such a long time. "You're a beautiful woman," my doctor began. "There's nothing wrong with your body. Your height and weight are proportionate, and you need to love the skin you're in."

She didn't really answer my question, but she made me see how much I was hurting myself with my distorted lens. Even though she was giving me a compliment, her words stung because I had to face that I had an emotional issue that needed to be addressed—one that involved beating myself up.

The truth is that my body dysmorphia was all too obvious to others. I realized that the day my twelve-year-old daughter said, "You're way too critical of yourself." It broke my heart. She watched me constantly look for small flaws, tearing myself apart.

Shortly after that doctor's appointment, I took my daughter to a concert, and we decided to buy the CD produced by Mister Wives, the opening band. On the cover, the band was pictured as animals, and each animal represented one band member's "spirit animal." One of them was a squirrel, for example, and another was an elephant.

"I want to be the squirrel," I told my daughter. I thought that would be perfect, since squirrels are small and can hide easily.

"That beautiful elephant with the giant diamond is my favorite," my daughter said. "It must be the lead singer."

"No way," I responded. "She's so little and cute. I'll bet she's the squirrel."

"Mom, she's the only girl. None of the boys would be a pink-and-purple elephant with diamonds and jewels."

Clearly, my daughter was light years ahead of me even then.

I was overcome with shame at the thought that I wanted to be the smallest animal so that I wouldn't attract a lot of attention. My child was so right—the singer's actual size may have been small, but she had a larger-than-life personality and was living in three dimensions. I was reminded in that moment that size doesn't matter at all. What matters is how we feel about ourselves and how we choose to present ourselves in the world.

I got another important lesson one morning while practicing yoga. I caught a glimpse of my arms in a mirror. There's something about the way the skin of the upper arms hangs . . . and the cellulite. It just horrified me. A friend likes to remind me that no one walks around with their arms in the goal-post position, waving them in the air, but I still wanted my arms to look amazing in a tank top and bathing suit.

But while I was doing my yoga poses, I decided to turn away from obsessing about my arms. I went into a "crow pose," which is a balancing yoga pose that can be challenging to learn and do. As I set up the pose, I made sure to put a blanket on the floor in front of me in case I fell face-forward. I slowly placed my weight on my arms and glanced into the mirror. What I saw shocked me. It was the first time I realized that this beautiful pose was the answer to my body dysmorphia about my arms! There they were, able to hold the entire weight of my body off the ground.

For the first time, I saw my arms in a much different light. "Wow, these arms can hold up my 125 pounds and stay balanced," I thought. "They're really strong, and strong is beautiful!"

Changing Your Perceptions about Your Body

So much of the body dysmorphia battle is about perception. However, I'm not going to pretend that healing dysmorphia is as easy as taking a pill. It's another lifelong journey that requires you to be vigilant about the way you talk to yourself, catching yourself in distorted perceptions and correcting yourself in the moment.

The truth is that regardless of your size, you might struggle to see yourself realistically. My friend Sarah told me a story about her friend Robin, who had struggled with anorexia and was still very thin. They were at a party, and Sarah observed Robin looking in a mirror, saying, "I look fat."

Sarah was floored. How could Robin ever think she was fat? Sarah wasn't fat either, but she was considerably larger than Robin. So she stood next to Robin so that they could both be seen in the mirror.

"Robin, do you think I'm fat?" Sarah asked.

Robin immediately said. "No, not at all!"

"Well, look at how much bigger I am than you. If *I'm* not fat, how could *you* possibly be fat?"

Robin just stood there for a moment, stunned. It was an eye-opener for her.

The truth is that how you talk about yourself *to* yourself creates your reality. But as we've already established, the only way to stop the self-hating chatter is to become aware of it and be vigilant about it. I found that it helped me to remind my friends when they made self-deprecating remarks. "You aren't stupid," I'd say with a gentle hand on my friend's shoulder. Or "No, you aren't fat; please stop being mean to my friend," I'd say to another. This helped me to begin to treat myself with the same kindness.

Here's another way to get a handle on the negative psychobabble in your head. To break the pattern, put a quarter in a jar every time you say something self-defeating or cruel about yourself, either out loud or in your mind. If you're like me, you'll be amazed at how quickly you can grow a vacation fund! (Paris, anyone?) That's not all: dropping the quarters in the jar forces you to become mindful of how often you put yourself down.

I also became mindful of how I speak to myself when I look in the mirror. The impulse was to immediately pick my body apart and put myself down. I had to take a deep breath and just stop. I thought about how I would greet a stranger. Would I be likely to pick that person's body apart, or would I simply greet her with a pleasant, "Hello! How are you?"

I started to treat myself in the mirror the way I would treat a stranger. Try it. Look in the mirror, and pretend you don't know the person looking back at you. You're going to be polite to this person. You want this person to like you, and you never know if you might make a new friend, right? Treating yourself the way you would treat someone else is one of the best ways I know to stop the self-hatred habit.

The bottom line is that you deserve the same kindness that you'd give another person. And if you *are* having harsh thoughts about other people's bodies, know that this is a reflection of how you feel about yourself. Even if your body is very different from theirs, whatever you say to yourself about them reflects your fears. I'll bet you're equally as harsh to yourself, so the time is now to create a new habit of being kind to others and to yourself.

Exercise: How to Find Soft-Focus Vision

I had a Rolfing instructor who tried to get me to see the human form in soft focus. At first, I couldn't figure out what she meant. But we were in Colorado, so I said, "You mean with 'stoner' eyes?"

She burst out laughing. "Yes, something like that."

The trick to finding your soft-focus eyes is to close your eyes about halfway. Try it:

1. Stand in front of the mirror (clothed or naked—either is fine). What's the first thing you notice about yourself? Are there body parts that you think are too big, misshapen, or otherwise unpleasing? Are there body parts you like better than others?

2. Now, soften your vision by closing your eyes about halfway. Does your perspective change? Pretend that this way of looking at yourself is the equivalent to wearing "rose-colored glasses." Are you no longer looking at your body as if through a microscope, trying to find every tiny flaw?

3. Now, think about all that your body does for you each day. It gets you from place to place. It carries things for you. It gives you pleasure. It provides your senses with so much experience. What a gift, regardless of how it looks or whatever deficits it might have. As you look at your body in soft focus, thank it for all it has done for you, and apologize for treating it unkindly.

Alternate Nostril Breathing Exercise

This breathing exercise is a great way to begin to change your perspective. It helps you integrate the right and left sides of your brain and can help calm your nervous system. If you struggle to meditate, it can be helpful to do this when you start any meditation practice.

1. Gently place your right thumb on your right nostril (without pressing the nostril closed), and rest your index and middle finger gently on your forehead (third eye area). Rest your ring and pinky fingers on your left nostril (without pressing the nostril closed).
2. Without closing either nostril, take three deep breaths, inhaling and exhaling.
3. Gently close your right nostril with your thumb as you breathe in through your left nostril while counting from one to four.
4. Release your right nostril, and use your ring and pinky fingers to close your left nostril as you gently exhale through your right nostril, counting from one to four.
5. Inhale to a count of one to four through your right nostril, and gently close the right side as you exhale to a count of one to four through your left nostril.
6. Repeat steps three through six at least five times.

If you can, do this as many as ten times in a row with your left arm propping up your right arm. When you start to get used to this, try using your other hand. (If you're left-handed, you may wish to start with your left hand.)

Generally, this is a calming exercise, but there have been times when I have had anger come up. If that happens for you, take a break, and allow yourself to express the anger in a safe way. If the anger isn't intense, you might just be able to breathe it out. Don't close either nostril, and imagine that the anger is being released with each exhale.

Meditation:
Quieting the Voice That Says You Have to Be "Perfect"

This meditation will help you let go of the need to be perfect.

1. Find a comfortable space where you can sit on the floor or in a chair with your feet flat on the floor. Make sure you will have quiet with as few distractions as possible. Turn the ringer all the way off on your phones!

2. Once you're comfortable in your seated position, close your eyes and begin to focus on your breathing. Inhale through your nose, and exhale through your mouth. Can you hear and feel the rise and fall of your breath? To help you inhale and exhale for about the same duration, count from five to one on each inhale and from five to one on each exhale. Feel your rib cage expand as you inhale and contract as you exhale. Try to fill your lungs and diaphragm with your breath all the way to the bottom of your rib cage.

3. Now take a moment to clear your mind. This is the hardest part, so don't worry if you find it difficult! Even monks who have been meditating for decades can find this difficult. Each time a thought enters your mind, just allow it to float away, and come back to yourself.

4. Think about the flaws you see in your body. Choose the flaw that bothers you the most, and concentrate on it for a moment. Imagine that this flaw belongs to someone else you love. As you see the flaw on your loved one, do you notice it? Or does it fade into the background? Is this a flaw that needs to be let go of, or is it inconsequential when it belongs to someone you love?

5. Now come back to seeing this flaw on your own body, and imagine that another culture considers this flaw to be the

most beautiful thing a body could possibly have. For example, let's say you hate your round belly. What if round bellies are the height of beauty in this other culture? Truly imagine what that would be like! Can you see your belly from this perspective? Smile at this body part on which you're focused, and allow yourself to laugh at the absurdity of expecting everyone to look the same.

6. Thank this body part for teaching you about acceptance, and send love to this perceived "flaw."

7. Imagine that every negative thought you've ever had about yourself is in front of you in a big clump, sort of like a big ball of yarn. Now, picture a door in your mind's eye—it can be as small as a closet door or as large as a massive entryway to a mansion. Imagine that you open the door, and behind the door is a huge cauldron of boiling liquid. Place that big ball of negative thoughts in the cauldron, and watch for a few moments as they boil into nothing. Then either slam the door shut or close it gently, whichever you prefer. I find it helpful to put a lock on the door because I know I don't ever want to visit those thoughts again!

8. Remember that the intention of these negative thoughts was to try to keep you safe, maybe to make sure you were perfect enough to be loved. But those thoughts were misguided, and they no longer serve a purpose.

9. Once all of your darkness is safely boiled away behind the locked door, you can forgive yourself for all of those thoughts. See yourself as the small child you were, a child who didn't know any better than to try to be perfect in

order to be loved. Feel compassion in your heart for that child. Let the tears come if they do. They're healing.

10. See yourself as a child in your mind's eye and say, "I'm sorry, and I forgive myself." You may want to add "I love you" to this small child who is you.

11. When you're ready to come out of the meditative state, gently allow your mind to come back to the room, feel the sensation of the chair beneath you, feel your feet connected to the ground, and feel the space above your head gently expand. Slowly open your eyes and take a soft-focus view of the room. Allow your mind to come back to present time but hold on to the feeling of acceptance.

12. As you continue through your day, remember that your flaws make you unique, and everyone is "perfectly imperfect."

The Path to Self-Forgiveness

One night after my weight-loss surgery, I ate too much. I knew it right away. There was this sick, uneasy feeling in my throat, and I couldn't swallow. I struggled to breathe and started to panic, but the food finally went down.

It was a tasting dinner with four courses, and this had to happen on the very first dish! I felt so guilty. Why would I go to an expensive dinner when my stomach was now the size of a baby's? I would have been better off taking that money and applying it to something I really wanted to do rather than going along with what my companion wanted. As a consequence of my determined people-pleasing skills, I ended up sitting there not even tasting the rest of the food!

While the remainder of the meal was served, I silently berated myself. *See, Nicole, you have no self-control, no will-power. You're doomed to be an overeater forever. You'll be just like those people who regain all their weight after weight-loss surgery.*

I excused myself to the bathroom, where I looked in the mirror. Suddenly, I realized that one mistake at one meal shouldn't doom me to a life of failure. This time, I silently thought, *Nicole, I forgive you for making this choice tonight. You now know what happens when you eat too much, so you won't do it again.*

I knew in my heart that from that day forward, I would forgive myself more and question myself less. But like most people, self-forgiveness has been a struggle for me. Why is it so much easier to forgive other people for their mistakes and imperfections?

Like most everything, self-forgiveness is a practice. It isn't something you learn once and then you're done. You have to keep it up on a daily basis by catching yourself when you start to beat yourself up. Each time is an opportunity to forgive yourself. As you catch yourself more and more, you can immediately say, either silently or aloud "Stop!" Interrupt that voice!

It might be difficult to get that voice to stop at first, but you just have to keep saying "Stop!" over and over. As I've gotten better at it, self-forgiveness has helped me not just forgive myself for certain behaviors, but also to heal my body dysmorphia. It has allowed me to forgive myself for not being perfect.

When you talk to yourself, ask yourself these questions: 1) Is what I've just said to myself kind and loving, and 2) does it serve my higher purpose? If you can't answer "yes" to both of these questions, you need to change the way you speak to yourself. You need to take the opportunity to forgive yourself—first for whatever you're berating yourself about, and second for beating yourself up about it.

Try this: Imagine that you're on a drawbridge, and the gates are up because they're allowing a ship to pass underneath. You're at a standstill. You can't move forward or backward because there are people behind you. While you're stopped, ask yourself why you're so hard on yourself. You can write the answer down, or you can just answer it in your mind. Are you afraid that if you aren't hard on yourself, you'll never be perfect? And if you aren't perfect, are you afraid other people might not love you? That's a common fear, but it's also irrational, isn't it? No one is perfect, and other people sometimes can't love you because they have the same fear and self-hatred inside that prevents them from loving.

Whatever your answer is, know that you're going to leave that fear or belief on the drawbridge. As soon as the gates come back down and you can drive across the bridge to the other side, you'll leave that nonsense belief on the bridge.

Do this every time you catch yourself beating yourself up, and eventually, you won't need to stop on the drawbridge nearly as much! You'll be able to forgive yourself for being the imperfect human being you have every right to be.

Exercise: Letter to Yourself

In this exercise, you'll write a love letter to yourself, forgiving yourself for whatever you blame yourself for and offering yourself the encouragement you need. If this is difficult for you, imagine that you're writing a letter forgiving and encouraging someone else—someone you feel truly deserves your forgiveness.

After you've written the letter, read it again, and really try to let it in. Here's my letter to myself as an example:

> *Dear Nicole,*
>
> *It has taken me a long time to write this letter, and I fear it's one of the hardest I will ever write. To anyone. You see, long ago, a series of events happened that changed the direction of your life. And I know there have been countless times you've wondered "what if?" What if things had been different? What would my life be like now? Would I have the same friends? The same child? The same life? Just without the memory of trauma? And the honest answer is "yes."*
>
> *Yes, your life would have been different. But different in what way? There are no guarantees in life, so you may have experienced something far worse. In the end, it doesn't matter, because you can't go back and change the past. Remember the old saying about the four things you can't take back—the word after it's spoken, the stone after it's thrown, the action after it's done, and the time that has passed. So please, please stop worrying about what has happened, and recognize some of your accomplishments.*
>
> *I have watched you take shape as a human being and grow and change in ways that I wouldn't have thought possible if I hadn't been there myself to witness it. It pains me deeply that for so many years,*

you felt the need to question every single decision you made. And I hope upon endless hope that you learn to trust yourself. Because it doesn't matter which choice you make. Each choice will have its own special outcome, and that's a good thing.

The future hasn't happened, so there's no need to worry if things will work out. They will work out exactly the way they're supposed to, and you don't have to do anything to help the process.

For too long, I watched and listened to you put yourself down and say mean things to yourself, and as your truest friend in this lifetime, I have to ask you to please stop. Stop doing this forever and ever. It isn't cute, and it isn't funny to be self-deprecating. It's a mask of your pain, and you don't need that shield anymore. You have faced all that scares you, and you've come out ahead of it. You're a strong, intelligent, beautiful, capable woman, and you have your whole life ahead of you.

Please know that you're going to hit a lot of speed bumps in the future. It doesn't mean that the world is coming to an end. In fact, I would say you should welcome those speed bumps, as they're going to be your greatest teachers. A wise person once told me that I wouldn't know how strong I really was and what I was really made of until I didn't have any other choice than to be strong. So go out into this world and be the woman warrior you are. Embrace your life, and live each moment in the present.

On the day you were born, there was an earth-quake in Santa Monica, and the only window in the hospital that cracked was the one in your room. Your dad always said he thought it was an auspicious start to your life. And it was! Make every moment count, and be kind to everyone, even if they don't deserve it. I love you fiercely, and I'm your greatest cheerleader. I forgive you everything because there's truly NOTH-ING TO FORGIVE. When you feel down, read this letter, and remember you're strong. You can do this!

Love always,
Nicole

MINDFUL MOMENT

It's very easy to get stuck in a rut, especially when you have body dysmorphia. You get stuck in the rut of believing your body has to look a certain way, and it can be difficult to get unstuck. Think about how hard it is to get a vehicle out of mud. The tires spin endlessly, while the motor works overtime to try to move. You have to find something to put under the tire that will enable it to gain traction.

Just like when your car is stuck in the mud, you have to put a new thought in your head to help you gain traction so you can drive away from the onslaught of your negative thoughts. To help yourself stop spinning your wheels with negativity, make yourself a "Get out of sad quick card," or tell yourself a sweet story that you remember reading. Read your forgiveness letter to yourself. Most of all, forgive yourself for getting stuck sometimes. It's happened to me many times, and it happens to everyone. Each time, find a way to get traction and get yourself unstuck, knowing that you'll probably get stuck in the mud again some other time.

chapter six

GIVING UP THE VICTIM AND BLAME GAME

You may have been challenged, hurt, betrayed, beaten, and discouraged, but nothing has defeated you. You are still here! You have been delayed but not denied. You are not a victim, you are a victor. You have a history of victory.
—Steve Maraboli

Many years ago, I pulled a muscle in my leg and couldn't exercise for a while. Within five months, I gained sixty-five pounds. It was so easy for me to say the weight gain wasn't my fault, but the truth is that I wasn't controlling my eating during that five months. It was the "poor, pitiful me syndrome." *If only I wasn't injured, I wouldn't be so heavy.*

I loved trying to get sympathy, but false sympathy is as poor a substitute for love as food. I was playing the victim card for all it was worth.

One friend tried to call me out on my victim role. While watching me eat ice cream and listening to me complain about my weight gain, she said, "Well, what kind of food choices are you making?"

"It doesn't matter because I'm injured!" I snapped back at her.

I just didn't want to take responsibility for my actions. That's what we do when we play the victim.

Of course, I want to make a clear distinction between "playing" the victim and actually being a victim. When I was raped at fourteen, I was absolutely a victim. I had no control over what happened to me. But let's be clear: Even with an injury, I wouldn't have gained sixty-five pounds in five months if I had eaten more carefully. I knew what would happen if I ate too much, but I just didn't want to face that. It was easier to pretend that it was all due to my pulled muscle. It was easier to throw a tantrum and say, "The world is out to get me!"

It could be that the rape set me up to feel that the world was out to get me, but eventually, we have to let go of whatever difficult circumstances life has given us and hold ourselves accountable for the results we get. How long can we say, "If only I'd had better parents" or "If only my parents had stayed together" or "If only my parents had gotten divorced" or, in my case, "If only I hadn't been raped"? I don't say that to be harsh. I have nothing but compassion for the pain that anyone has experienced in their lives.

But once you've dealt with the trauma (which does require considerable healing of the mind, the spirit, and the body), you can create the life you want only if you're willing to burn the victim card and take responsibility for the results you get in your life.

The rape happened to me, and it certainly had an effect on me. Even if it altered me in significant ways, it still isn't who I am. It didn't define my personhood or turn me into a victim in every aspect of my life. Think about it: When you ask yourself, "Who am I?" the last answer you want to give is, "I'm a victim."

It's a cop-out to blame your inaction or negative behavior on something other than yourself. By playing victim, you give your power away, and you rob yourself of the ability to create what you want. When you take that power back, you have to let go of blaming your life's circumstances for your lack of results. You then have to actually try to change your life and risk failing in the process. It's scary—I know!

That's why everyone plays the victim at some point in his or her life. We all want to wallow in feeling sorry for ourselves, and we want to avoid falling on our faces. But every successful person fails many times before he or she succeeds.

The *only* result from playing the victim is that you get to stay the victim without ever finding out what you're capable of. You never get to change your circumstances. You get to live only half a life.

When you take back your power, the possibilities are infinite. You have the opportunity to do anything. Yes, you'll probably fail a few times, but that's part of what living a full life means. The risk is well worth it.

Healthy Emotions versus Playing the Victim

It's important to make another distinction about victimhood. Feeling sad isn't the same as playing the victim. You can feel sad for what you've experienced and even feel sorry for yourself to some degree, but as long as you don't make excuses for not taking responsibility for your life, you *aren't* playing the victim. If you're releasing painful feelings rather than wallowing in them, you're taking steps toward healing.

It's healthy to feel your emotions. Asking for support from others is also healthy. You aren't playing the victim, for example, when you allow yourself to express your vulnerability and ask a friend to be there for you. You're in your power when you ask for what you need. It takes courage to be vulnerable and ask others to help. You aren't making excuses when you do that. You're taking good care of yourself!

Exercise: What Are Your Excuses?

You may not be aware of all of the times you play the victim, so simply think about the times you feel defeated. In what areas of your life do you feel that you can't get a leg up? Where have you given up? What do you say to yourself and/or to others about why you can't accomplish what you want?

1. Write down whatever excuses you can think of—even if you're entirely convinced that they're all out of your control. For example, you might write, "I can't start the business I want because I don't have the money" or "I can't find anyone to date because I've been divorced twice" or "I can't lose weight because my job is sedentary."

   It's true that you might have true challenges. It could be that starting a business would be difficult for you because of your financial situation, but if you put your mind to it, you might be able to come up with a strategy to get around that obstacle. Think about the people you've read about who have overcome much worse obstacles and odds. If they can do it, so can you. It's all about taking back your power and not allowing your victim energy to defeat you before you even try . . . or even if you fail a couple of times on the road to reaching your goal, I can guarantee you one thing: *The victim energy will defeat you much more than any circumstances in your life.*

2. After you've written down your list of excuses, read them again, thinking of them as obstacles that you can overcome. Choose the one that you'd like to act on the most, and write down one action that you can take to begin to step right over that obstacle.

If you want to start a business but don't have the capital, maybe the first action would be to create a budget to lower your spending and put a small amount of money away each week toward your goal. The second action might be to join a group in your area with other entrepreneurs to find out how they started their own businesses.

Resistance to Receiving Good Things

One of the reasons you stay in victim mode is that you don't believe you deserve good things. Once again, it all comes down to self-love. The more you love yourself, the more you want to step outside of your fear and take on the challenges to create the life you want. If your self-love is weak, you'll easily "fall victim" to your own victim thinking. That's pretty ironic, huh? But victim thinking is a product of low self-esteem, and when you don't have faith in yourself and what you can accomplish, you don't take the steps to follow your dreams. Then you blame your fate on everything but your own inaction.

When you don't love yourself, you actually resist receiving good things. You might even be so good at giving to others that you don't know how to receive. You feel uncomfortable when someone gives you a gift or a compliment. Notice how you feel when someone gives you a present or says something nice about you. Do you feel that you deserve it, or do you act like it isn't warranted?

In our culture, you're probably constantly coming up against the conflict of what you've been taught about receiving. On the one hand, you're taught that it isn't good to want too much. You shouldn't be greedy. You shouldn't want when so many people have so little. The last thing you want is to be like the greedy corporations you read about in the news, and some part of you is afraid you'd run amuck if you let yourself want even a little bit.

You've probably also been taught that you can create your own abundance and that wanting is a good thing. You set an example for others when you allow yourself to live abundantly. You deserve it, and you can have what you want if you only believe.

The truth and your comfort level probably reside somewhere in between those conflicting lessons. You don't have to go to extremes, but most of us do without realizing it as we barely allow ourselves to receive much at all.

Here's some homework that you can do on a regular basis: Practice accepting kindnesses and gifts from others with the knowledge that you deserve what you're being given. Think about how you feel when you say something nice to someone else or when you give someone a gift. It feels good, especially if the other person is appreciative. So give the other person the return gift of your appreciation without acting as though you aren't worthy of it. In a moment, we're going to do a meditation to open your heart to yourself, and that will help you with this homework. The meditation will also help you begin to open yourself to receiving more and more as your comfort level increases.

Think about the possibility that playing the victim is a compensation for your resistance to good things. When you tell others how terrible your life is, you might feel special in a strange way. Have you ever heard people compete over how bad they have it in life? (Maybe you've even entered into one of those competitions.) Who wants to win *that* contest? The payoff is feeling like you've won something, but it's quite a consolation prize, isn't it?

After my rape, I didn't feel I deserved anything, and I shut down from receiving. To a large degree, I felt unsafe accepting anything from anyone. If you feel that way, it's a clear indication that you still need to do some post-trauma healing work. While there's a lot a book can do for you, that kind of healing requires professionals who work with you one-on-one. Please do everything you can to heal your trauma so that you can get past the belief that you don't deserve. I'm here to tell you that this is a false belief, and a better life is waiting for you. To the best of your ability, allow yourself to receive all that's good.

Exercise: Permission Slip

Write out the following permission slip for yourself to receive all that the universe is capable of giving you. Feel free to revise it and make it your own!

> I, _____ [fill in your name], hereby give myself permission to accept more goodness in my life. I give myself permission to take in compliments, knowing that they are truths about me. I give myself permission to accept gifts from others graciously, knowing that I deserve them and that giving the gift to me provides pleasure to the giver. I give myself permission to accept more and more gifts from the universe, and I take each one with gratitude, knowing that there's always more, and that by taking my share, I'm not taking away from anyone else. The abundance of the universe is infinite. And so it is.

Meditation: Open to Receive

We often find it easy to open our hearts to others but not to ourselves. This meditation is designed to help you open your heart to *you*. Then you will open it to allow the universe to give you blessings, kindness, love, and abundance.

1. Sit in a comfortable chair with your feet planted firmly on the ground. Rest your arms at your sides, on top of your thighs or on the arms of the chair.
2. Close your eyes, and feel the earth beneath your feet. Feel how it supports you.
3. Begin by relaxing your body as best you can by starting at the bottom of your feet and moving up to the top of your head. Take as long as you need with this part of the meditation. Just command each part of your body to relax, and as you move up higher and higher, each part will relax more.
4. Now, take all of the love that you feel for others, and center it in your heart. Let it get bigger and bigger. How much love do you feel for the special people and animals in your life? See that love represented as a beautiful light in your heart. Maybe it's white or pink or green, or maybe it's a rainbow of colors.
5. Imagine turning that light of love in your heart toward yourself. Let the light travel throughout your body— through your shoulders and down your arms, up toward your neck and head, down toward your lower torso, and down your legs to the bottoms of your feet. This love is who you are. Let it fill every inch of you. Know that you're

as deserving of this love as the others in your life. Bask in this love and light as long as you want.

6. Now, imagine that the light in your heart area is opening like a flower in the center of your chest. Instead of sending that love outward, imagine that you are receiving love and blessings from the universe into your heart with each inhalation. Breathe in, and take more of that love into your heart. As you breathe out, allow that love to travel throughout your body. Breathe in and out several times. You're being filled with your own love and the love of the universe. How much can you allow yourself to take in? There's a limitless amount of love you can have. Take all that you can. You can come back and do this meditation again and again to expand the amount that you allow yourself to receive.

7. When you're ready, begin to come back from your meditative state by wiggling your fingers and toes. Gently let your head roll from side to side. Open your eyes slowly and look around until you feel fully awake.

8. Keep the love and light throughout your body for as long as you possibly can.

Accepting Other People As They Are

We've already talked about fat shaming and how cruel other people can be. And we've talked about how their cruelty is an expression of their own pain. But when others are mean to you, it's very difficult not to feel like a victim, isn't it? It's still a challenge for me after all these years of working on it.

I think you'll find that the more you love yourself, the less you'll receive unkind comments from others. The more self-love you develop, the more you attract loving people. But there will still be times when someone will say something, either inadvertently or purposely, that hurts you. Life is just like that sometimes, no matter how much you work on yourself.

The more you put yourself out into the world, the more likely you'll experience unkind comments. As I write this book, I know there's a good chance I'm going to get a bad review or two (or three or more). I don't want to go into a victim space every time I read one, so I have to come to a place of acceptance that other people will be who they are and do what they do. I have to accept that I have no power to change or control others. The only power I have is to center myself in my own self-loving to the best of my ability and know that such comments are unimportant.

Have you ever read *The Four Agreements* by Don Miguel Ruiz? One of the agreements is to not take anything personally. This is a difficult one, but the more I remind myself of it, the better I get at fulfilling that agreement. As some people say, what someone else thinks of you is really none of your business.

So as you work on letting go of the victim mentality, I invite you to remind yourself of that agreement every time someone's words sting you. *Don't take it personally.* No matter how much it seems like it is personal, it really isn't. It's all about that other person's stuff. If someone points out something you think you really need to work on, fine. Work on it. But do your best not to beat yourself up for not being perfect.

Helping Others from an Empowered Place

If you truly have a difficult time feeling that you deserve good things, practice kindness to others. We've already talked about this a bit, but in this context, it will help you feel positive and less victimized.

Of course, I'm not advising that you be a people-pleaser or give over to codependency. I'm talking about giving to others from an empowered place. It's easy to just be friendly and kind to people you meet during your day. Even if you're an introvert, you can extend yourself to some degree.

If you have the time and inclination, you can do volunteer work as a way of "earning" the goodness that comes into your life. Just know that this is a mind trick you're playing on yourself because the truth is that you don't have to earn good things. Nevertheless, if telling yourself you have earned what you receive helps you to open yourself up to receiving more, it's okay in the beginning. As you start to allow more goodness into your life, remind yourself that you don't have to do anything to merit that goodness. Connect more and more with how much you deserve it simply by being yourself and doing the best you can in your life.

Meditation:
Let Go of the Victim and Step into Empowerment

In this meditation, we'll work on letting go of the victim inside and step into the empowered person you're becoming.

1. Sit in a comfortable chair with your feet planted firmly on the ground. Rest your arms at your sides, on top of your thighs or on the arms of the chair.

2. Close your eyes, and begin to relax your body as best you can by starting at the bottom of your feet and moving up to the top of your head. Take as long as you need with this part of the meditation. Just command each part of your body to relax, and as you move up higher and higher, each part will relax more.

3. See yourself as the wounded and hurt child you were. In your mind's eye, imagine yourself hugging your child self, giving this part of you all the love you can muster. Feel compassion for the parts of you who have felt like a victim.

4. The time has come, however, to leave the victim mindset behind. You have the power to create the life you want, but only if you take responsibility for your choices and take actions toward your dreams.

5. In your mind's eye, see a door in front of you. In a moment, you're going to open this door and step into your future. That future you will leave the victim behind. This new you has the courage to take responsibility for yourself and move toward the life you want to create. You'll feel afraid sometimes, but you won't let your fear stop you.

6. Take a deep breath, and open the door. Step through it, blowing a goodbye kiss to your victim self as you do.

7. Once you've stepped through the door, take another deep breath. What does it feel like to be this new empowered person? Close your eyes, and really feel it. This is the new you.

8. Victim mentality is a bad habit, so when you feel yourself backsliding to the other side of the door, close your eyes and picture yourself walking through that door into your empowered self again. Remember how you felt the first time you walked through the door.

9. When you're ready, begin to come back from your meditative state by wiggling your fingers and toes. Gently let your head roll from side to side. Open your eyes slowly and look around until you feel fully awake.

10. If possible, take a walk as your new empowered self. Does the world look different? How do you feel?

MINDFUL MOMENT

One of the most challenging things I ever had to do was allow myself to receive compliments from others. It took some time, but I learned to stop discounting the compliment and just say two words: "Thank you." I recommend stopping yourself when someone says something nice about you before you say, "Oh, this is an old outfit" or "I don't really sing all that well." Instead, just say, "Thank you," and allow the compliment in as much as you can. They meant it. Believe them!

chapter seven

THE ROAD TO HAPPINESS

Even a happy life cannot be without a measure of
darkness, and the word "happy" would lose its meaning
if it were not balanced by sadness.
—Carl Jung

Many years ago, I lived in the Caribbean. My friends and I often traveled to the British Virgin Islands for an afternoon aboard the Willy T, which was a floating bar in the middle of nowhere. There was an upper deck that had views for days and a small platform that people jumped from into the warm waters of the Caribbean Sea.

I could never seem to build up the courage to make that jump off the side of the boat, though. And one of my biggest regrets is that I let fear intimidate me when I knew it wasn't really dangerous.

Fast forward to a vacation in Kauai last summer, and I found myself on a snorkel trip to the forbidden island. We weren't going to step onto the forbidden island, but we would be able to see it clearly and swim in the clear blue waters next to it. As

I was standing on the boat fiddling around with my snorkel gear, I heard the captain yell out, "This is the oldest and the youngest you're ever going to be. Tomorrow isn't promised to anyone, so if there is something you want to do today, do it!" As soon as he said that, I knew I was going to gather my courage and jump off the boat.

But when I got to the side ready to jump, my fear kicked in again even though I could tell it was only about a ten-foot drop. I asked myself, "What's the worst thing that can happen?" I counted to ten, held my nose, screamed, and just jumped. As I flew through the air, hit the water, and rose back to the surface, I screamed loudly. But it wasn't because I was afraid. It was because I was excited.

I loved it so much that I did it again!

When I told my twelve-year-old daughter about it, she couldn't believe it. And I had to pinch myself to believe I'd actually done it.

What held me back for so long? What had I really been so afraid of? I still don't know for sure, but I can tell you that facing my fears that day was one of the strongest acts of courage I have ever experienced. It helped me see myself in a new way, and I've never been the same. That one action increased my courage many times over, and even though fear comes up again, it will never quite have the strength it had before I jumped off that boat!

What about you? What have you always wanted to do but haven't managed to muster the courage to do?

In my opinion, a big part of happiness is having the courage to fulfill your dreams, no matter how big or small. Some dreams may be a tall order, but I'll bet there's a small dream you could fulfill soon if you think about it. One small act of courage can build more courage for something bigger. Then, more and more, you will fully show up in your life and participate in it with gusto and enthusiasm.

Exercise: Your Next Act of Courage

Here's an exercise to help you try a small act of courage.

1. Make a note of something you'd like to do that you haven't yet had the courage to do. If courage isn't your strong suit, it can be something relatively small. You don't have to jump off a boat! Maybe you'd like to ask someone you find interesting to lunch. Maybe it's even as small as saying hello to someone (which, depending on the circumstances, may not be small at all!) or posting a poem you wrote on social media.

2. Write a date in your calendar when you will have taken this act of courage. Don't give yourself more than a week to muster up your bravery. The longer you delay, the more likely you are to talk yourself of it.

3. If you find that you still can't quite get yourself to do it, run through the worst-case scenarios in your mind. Chances are they aren't as bad as you've made them out to be. For example, if you say hello to someone you like, and that person doesn't say hello back, what will happen? You might feel hurt, but you'll live. If you post a poem on social media, what's the likelihood that your friends will tell you it's terrible? If someone does that, how is that person your friend? So the worst that could probably happen is that no one comments at all. If you have some nice friends, this is unlikely.

Where Does Happiness Come From?

Well, that's the million-dollar question, isn't it? I'm not sure anyone can definitively answer that question. What I *am* certain of is that happiness is not some destination where you arrive and feel happy for the rest of your life. People say they want to be happy, but you can only feel happy in this moment. Then, the next. And the next. I believe happiness really involves stringing together as many moments of joy as you can during your life. You're not going to feel happy twenty-four/seven. At least I've never heard of anyone who has managed that. But I do believe you can achieve a kind of contentment and acceptance.

I want you to begin to open up to the possibility of having more joyful moments. Some people are so cut off from joy that they don't even know what might help them feel it. Or they just never stopped to think about it. For others, joyful moments are tainted by pervasive fears that don't allow them to fully let go into the experience. They're so afraid of what *might* happen that they can't enjoy what *is* happening. Or their self-esteem is so low that they don't allow themselves to feel joy because they don't believe they deserve it. I hope I'm not describing you, but if I am, take heart. You can learn to experience joy more fully, and as you know, this book is all about helping you to love yourself more and let go of fear (or at least feel the fear and do it anyway, as the saying goes). It might take work for you to learn how to feel joyful, but you can do it! I know you can. Look—you're reading the words of someone who was raped as a teenager, tried to commit suicide, spent time in mental institutions to heal from all of that trauma, and came out the other side of obesity. If I can learn to experience joy, anybody can.

If you're like many others, you might think joy is something you can only feel during the special times in life, like when you graduate, get married, or have a baby. But the more you learn how to appreciate and experience joy through the simple things in life, the more you can piece together moments of happiness that flow without so many interruptions. In other words, you can learn to sustain feelings of happiness and joy longer if you find joy in everyday experiences.

Think about some of the small things that can bring joy. Your child's laughter. A favorite song. Flowers. Animals. Babies. Art and architecture. If you take stock of your favorite things, you can make it a regular habit to partake of them (if you're struggling with your weight, that probably shouldn't include food). Some things might cost you money, but listening to your favorite song, noticing children who are outside playing, visiting a free museum, smelling flowers, or spending time in nature shouldn't cost you a thing. (If you need more ideas, revisit "Take Good Care of #1" list in chapter 2.)

Let's take stock of your favorites and make a plan to fill your life with more joy and happiness, even—or especially—if you're going through something painful.

Exercise: Your Joy List

If you keep this joy list handy, it can be your "Get Out of Sad Quick" card. You can also simply refer to it often to remind yourself to "smell the roses" and make sure you have plenty of moments when you appreciate what brings you joy. For example, if you're a grandmother who gets the most joy from spending time with your grandchildren, can you spend time with them more often? If they're not nearby, can you at least Facetime or Skype with them more?

1. Make a list of your favorite things. Think about everything from people to places to food to music to objects.

2. Go back over your list and place a star by anything that's in your life on a regular basis. How often do you appreciate the presence of these things and really savor them?

3. Make a pact with yourself that you will (1) seek out more moments with your favorite things and (2) savor the time you have with them, experiencing everything about them fully, using all five of your senses.

Meditation: Finding Joy

1. Find a comfortable space where you can sit on the floor or in a chair with your feet flat on the floor. Choose a quiet place with as few distractions as possible. Turn the ringer all the way off on your phones!

2. Once you're comfortable in your seated position, close your eyes, and begin to focus on your breathing. Inhale through your nose and exhale through your mouth. Can you hear and feel the rise and fall of your breath? To help you inhale and exhale for about the same duration, count from five to one on each inhale and from five to one on each exhale. Feel your rib cage expand as you inhale and contract as you exhale. Try to fill your lungs and diaphragm with your breath all the way to the bottom of your rib cage.

3. Now take a moment to clear your mind. Each time a thought enters your mind, just allow it to float away, and come back to yourself.

4. Ask yourself: When have I felt pure, unadulterated joy in my life? Allow your mind to show you a memory of a joyful experience you've had. It might be a moment you shared with a loved one, parent, sibling, or friend. Perhaps you were swinging on a swing with your legs gently pumping back and forth to enable you to go faster.

5. If you can't recall a moment of pure joy in your life, make one up, perhaps from when you were very young. Just imagine it! What do you imagine would bring you joy?

6. Hear your own laughter, and try to bring on that feeling of joy to the best of your ability. Engage all your senses: imagine or remember the smells, tastes, sights, sounds, and textures. Allow that feeling of joy to fill you up from head to toe. Can you imagine your entire body filled with joy? Can you then allow that pure joy to spread outside your body? Can you imagine it going all the way to the top of the sky? Can you feel it hitting the ground beneath your feet? Can you feel the joy spreading to all corners of the universe? Imagine that your joy is making the world more joyful as you feel it and remember it. Stay in this feeling for as long as you like.

7. When you're ready, feel your body again; wiggle your shoulders and toes. Feel the sensation of the chair beneath you, and slowly open your eyes. Look at the room with a soft focus, and slowly bring your mind back to present time. Rub your arms and legs to help them wake up.

8. When you're ready, write down the sensations you experienced as best you can describe them. Write what you remembered and how it felt.

9. Keep what you've written, and the next time you're in a dark place, pull out your description to remember what joy is like. The more you practice bringing on this feeling at will, the better able you'll be to bring it on even when you're in the depths of despair. It may not remove all of the despair, but it will help to take the edge off of it and give you the strength to see another day.

Building Confidence from Within

Another important aspect of happiness is self-confidence. The more confident you feel about who you are and what you can do, the happier and more content you'll be on a regular basis. So how do you build your confidence so that you can be happy more frequently?

Again, it takes time. You aren't going to snap your fingers and suddenly feel self-confident. But the time to start is now. If you wait, you'll just prolong the wait. Here's my suggested six-step approach:

1. **Trust yourself:** I can say with some degree of certainty that I used to spend a lot of time questioning my own decisions. When you make a decision, own it. If it doesn't work out the way you imagined it would, do your best to trust that all will be okay. Failure is part of the process toward success.

2. **Be willing to change:** Think about the last time someone else drove your car and moved the seat from "your" position. Even small changes can be difficult, but they're important if you want to improve the quality of your life. Remind yourself of this every time you want to stick with the not-so-great familiar.

3. **Set goals:** The trick to setting goals is to make them realistic and attainable. It's a lot easier to set a goal for a five-pound weight loss than for a fifty-pound weight loss. If you break your goal into smaller pieces, you effectively "win" more often and faster. This internal mental reward system works wonders for your confidence in yourself.

4. **Expect the unexpected:** There will be people who leave your life for no good reason. Trust that when those doors close, others are opening for new friendships. It isn't a reflection on you or your worth when people leave.

5. **Believe in yourself:** No matter what you do, represent yourself the way you want others to see you. If you want to have long, pink hair, then do it. It really doesn't matter what anyone else thinks about it.

6. **Fake it till you make it:** If you don't feel confident, walk around as if you do. Be an actor, and pretend that you're someone you admire. It can do wonders for you to pretend, actually, because you're giving yourself a chance to feel what it's like to be confident. The more you do that, the more likely you'll be able to experience self-confidence regularly.

For me, confidence and happiness are two branches on the same tree. We can't truly be confident unless we are happy. When I have looked around at others who haven't been confident, one of the main things I see that helps to build confidence is to have a Confidence Buddy. This can be your best friend, spouse, or a trusted advisor, but it needs to be someone who always sees you through rose-colored glasses.

Again, confidence is something that takes time to build, so if it doesn't happen overnight, rest easy in the knowledge that everyone struggles with confidence at times.

Exercise: Happiness Contract

We've already talked about the importance of setting boundaries. One of the ways you can cultivate more happiness in your life is by saying "no" to what you don't want and "yes" to what you do want, as you've been learning in this chapter and the ones that came before.

Now let's make a contract to commit to finding joy and spending more time doing whatever you discover that makes you happy.

1. Copy the contract below and add your name to it, as you did with the Permission Slip in chapter 7. It may seem silly to do this, but writing it out really does help you to make a commitment.

2. Make any adjustments to the contract that you like in order to make it your own, or keep it as is. You might even want to post it somewhere in your home where you'll see it often.

> *I, _____, hereby commit to finding joy in the everyday things, appreciating what makes me happy, and savoring the moments of my life.*

Learning to Enjoy Your Own Company

I believe one of the keys to a happier life is learning to enjoy your own company. It's difficult when you don't love yourself: you just don't like yourself enough to feel that your own company is worth the time. Believe me, I know how painful that is. I'm not saying you should never want the company of others. We all need other people. That's just human nature. But the more you can learn to enjoy spending time alone, the happier you'll be because you'll be less dependent on others. So when you *are* alone, you'll be able to have a good time anyway, and you'll probably even begin to crave spending more time on your own.

How do you learn to enjoy spending time with yourself? Well, that takes time, and I believe if you do the work in this book, it will help you love and appreciate yourself more.

A big hurdle is stopping the negative self-talk. It's hard to spend time with your own thoughts if those thoughts are beating you up. When you get a handle on that self-talk, you'll be able to concentrate on the pleasure of your senses. You can sit on the beach and feel the wonderful damp air against your skin, smell the salt in the air, and feel the warm sand under your toes. You can sit quietly on the beach with a book and not have to entertain anyone else or answer their questions. And it will be bliss rather than loneliness or misery.

You can also think about the people in your life who do enjoy spending time with you. Think about the friends you've had in your life who asked you to go out with them or laughed at your jokes. I'll bet they're great people, so they know good company when they experience it. They must know something you don't!

No matter what, be patient with yourself as you work on building your love for yourself and quieting the punishing voice in your head. Slowly but surely, you'll get better at it and soon find that you actually enjoy sitting alone and doing exactly what you want to do without interference from anyone else.

MINDFUL MOMENT

Have you ever met someone who seemed happy all the time? You didn't trust them, did you? In fact, I'll bet they seemed like they were holding on to a lot of pain and anger underneath and were on the verge of blowing their top at any moment. The trick to happiness is to give over to the moment without thinking about the past or future. And know that no one else can be responsible for your happiness. It's your responsibility to find out what makes you happy and to seek it out.

chapter eight

YOU ARE BEAUTIFUL!

To me, beauty is about being comfortable in your own skin.
It's about knowing and accepting who you are.
—Ellen DeGeneres

A few years ago, after my surgery, I was invited to a fancy party. Well, let's just say that I don't normally do fancy parties. I'm usually wearing jeans. But I had to buy a nice outfit for this party, so I went to an upscale store.

I knew I didn't have an accurate view of how I look, so I thought I'd better get the help of a salesperson. (I used to think I looked good in overalls until my friend good-naturedly said, "Don't ever wear those again. You're too cute for those!")

The salesperson held out a dress and said, "This will look great on you!"

I looked at the label, and it was a size four. "I'm sure I'm not a four," I told her.

"You might be a two, but I'm pretty sure you're a four."

She thought I was convinced I was smaller than a four—but it was just the opposite! I assumed the size four would be too small for me.

I went into the dressing room and tried on the dress. *It fit*—I couldn't believe it. But I still wasn't sure if it looked good on me. So I walked out wearing the dress and looked for the salesperson to get her opinion.

As I was trying to find her, I caught the reflection of a woman in a very nice dress. In fact, she was wearing the same dress I was wearing.

Then it dawned on me. I was looking at myself. I didn't even recognize my own physical appearance.

It was a shock to me to realize that my image of myself was so false. I went home with my new dress and sat down with it in my hands for a few minutes, just thinking about how much I failed to see myself in the way others saw me. It was painful.

"You need to stop talking to yourself until you can be nice to yourself," I said. Then I remembered that when I was in my twenties, I lived with a man who was incredibly mean to me—physically, mentally, and emotionally. He was so abusive, in fact, that my neighbors noticed it and mentioned it to me. He constantly said, "You're fat, ugly, and stupid." The entire time I lived with him, that was my mantra about myself. And I carried that with me for a long time after.

"I need a new mantra," I said to myself as I felt the fabric of my new dress between my fingers. "Nobody else is ever going to tell me who I am. I know what I am and who I am."

So then and there, I created a new mantra that was meaningful to me: "I define my beauty." Just those four words—simple as that.

Think about it: Companies have a vision or mission statement. My mantra was my own personal mission statement, almost like asserting my personal brand.

The only way I could truly begin to live by that mantra and make it my own, though, was to put it in front of my face at every possible moment. It was my screensaver, on my phone, on my bathroom mirror—you name it.

Self-acceptance is difficult, especially if you've been living under a proverbial thousand-watt microscope of your own making. But there comes a time in your life when you have to say, "No one—not even me—will ever be allowed again to be a dimmer switch on my light." You get to choose how you show up for yourself and for the world. But you can't move forward if you keep putting yourself down.

As the title of this chapter says, you need to believe that *you are beautiful!* I don't care what you look like. I don't care if you live up to some silly standard of beauty that will change in the next twenty years. The reality is that you're going to be living with you for the rest of your life, so it's time to learn to love who you see in the mirror.

With that in mind, let's create your own personal mantra or mission statement to help you believe and remember your own beauty. You can borrow mine, if you like, or you can come up with one of your own.

Exercise: Your Personal Mantra

1. Close your eyes, and ask yourself for the most meaningful personal mantra you can imagine.

Sometimes an answer comes immediately, but not always. Sit for a few minutes and see if you get an idea.

2. If you aren't happy with what comes to mind, say the following before going to bed: "Please give me a mantra to help me see myself as beautiful." Then see if something comes to you by morning. You can ask this for a week and see if you hear a mantra that you love.

3. If, after a week, a mantra still hasn't come to you, make one up that you like, even if you don't adore it. You can always change your mantra later if you think of something you like better. But don't wait more than a week before you start working with your positive mantra.

4. Place your mantra everywhere you can so you see it over and over. Maybe even keep a paper clip in your pocket or wallet so that every time you put your hand there, you'll be reminded of your mantra. Bombard yourself with this mantra so that it becomes part of your DNA.

Triggers and Reactions

If you're like everyone else, every time you get hurt, it sets you up to try to avoid that same kind of hurt in the future. And you'll do almost anything to avoid that pain. You become highly sensitive to the possibility of experiencing that pain again. This is what triggers you at times to overreact.

Let's say your mother always made snide comments about how you dress. Then one day when your boyfriend says, "That's an interesting outfit," you go ballistic because you assume he's criticizing you. Meanwhile, he doesn't know what happened because he likes the outfit and meant nothing critical by his use of the word *interesting*. He might look at you and say, "You're touchy!" Your friends might think of you as "hypersensitive." That's all a result of emotional triggers.

You've probably been on the receiving end of a trigger, too, when a friend or family member reacts in a way that you don't understand after you did or said something you thought was perfectly innocent.

Everyone gets triggered at times, but the more you can become aware of your triggers and stop them in their tracks, the more peaceful your life will be. Your relationships will be more harmonious, too. In fact, the majority of arguments between people are based on these triggers.

How can you become aware of your triggers? The next time you become upset with someone, try to stop yourself from reacting automatically. Pause, take a deep breath, maybe count to the proverbial ten, and ask yourself if you might be making assumptions about what the other person meant or intended. Instead of jumping to conclusions, ask for clarification. Here's an example of what you might say: "Could you clarify your comment about _____? I want to make sure I fully understand what you meant."

Truthfully, the answer might trigger you again. So ask yourself: Is this related to something that happened to me in the past? How much of my anger belongs to the person in front of me, and how much belongs to a person from my past?

Think about times when you got very upset with someone. Was it a trigger? Be honest with yourself! Chances are it was.

I know how difficult it is to become aware of your triggers and not overreact, but the rewards of making this effort are enormous. You can save relationships and marriages if you work on becoming more aware of these triggers and learn to control your reactions a bit better.

I'm not suggesting, of course, that you block your emotions. But explosive emotions are usually best expressed in private rather than in the presence of another person. If you love the other person, you can do a lot of damage to your relationship if you allow yourself to explode.

Here's the bottom line: You have a choice in how you react to situations in your life. When you feel you've gotten the short end of the stick, you can wallow in that experience and react as though the universe is against you. Or you can remind yourself that everyone gets the short end of the stick at times. You can feel your sadness for a short time and then pick yourself up and try again. It's absolutely a choice.

Resilience, Perseverance, and Persistence

No matter what, you'll come up against a lot of obstacles in life. There's no avoiding it, so the best way I know to deal with life's challenges is to build your resilience. For me, resilience has been so much about self-love. When you get to a place where you love yourself better, you can withstand a great deal. You know that you deserve good things, and you know you *don't* deserve the ugliness that others try to put on you at times. You also know that you aren't being punished when something doesn't go your way. You realize that it's just a part of life.

You feel strong when you love yourself and when you see yourself as beautiful just because of who you are. It gives you an iron core that helps you stay standing like a tree that loses leaves and blows in the wind but remains tall with its trunk firmly planted.

When you're resilient, you can persevere. You can keep going even when you worry that you might not be able to. You don't want to give up on yourself, because you know you're worth it. So no matter how hard it may be, feel your pain, brush yourself off, and continue.

And as you persevere, you persist. You just refuse to give up. Years ago, I was a sales rep, and that job brought me the most rejection I'd ever experienced. I'd walk into offices or make calls, asking, "Do you need temporary staffing services?" The majority of the time, I heard, "No! Go away. Leave us alone."

But here's what happened: Within ten months after I started the job, I became the number-one sales rep for the company, and I held that title for three years. It showed me that even when you get rejected a lot, you can be successful. That's what persistence is all about. You keep going no matter what, and you don't allow outside circumstances to stop you.

I'm not saying that you don't allow yourself to be affected by anything. Of course you'll be affected by it. Feel all the feelings that the rejection brings up, but don't let those feelings be more powerful than you are. Let them out, and then get back up and try again. Remember that feelings move through you like visitors; soon enough, another feeling replaces the one that just passed by.

Every time you're resilient and you persevere, and persist, you'll build on those strengths and see yourself as stronger— much like I experienced after I jumped off that boat. You'll watch yourself handling more than you thought you could, and you'll find out that you're made of tougher stuff than you realized.

As Calvin Coolidge once said, "Nothing in this world can take the place of persistence. Talent will not nothing is more common than unsuccessful people with talent. Genius will not; unrewarded genius is almost a proverb. Education will not; the world is full of educated derelicts. Persistence and determination alone are omnipotent."

You deserve that kind of persistence. You're worth it. And you deserve to have a life as beautiful as you are.

Meditation: Creating a Protective Shield

In the first chapter, you visualized a protective light all around you. Let's build on that and create an even stronger protective shield that helps you stay strong regardless of what comes at you in life.

1. Find a comfortable space where you can sit on the floor or in a chair with your feet flat on the floor. Choose a quiet place with as few distractions as possible. Turn the ringer all the way off on your phones!

2. Once you're comfortable in your seated position, close your eyes and begin to focus on your breathing. Inhale through your nose and exhale through your mouth. Can you hear and feel the rise and fall of your breath? To help you inhale and exhale for about the same duration, count from one to five on each inhale and from five to one on each exhale. Feel your rib cage expand as you inhale and

contract as you exhale. Try to fill your lungs and dia-phragm with your breath all the way to the bottom of your rib cage.

3. Now take a moment to clear your mind. Each time a thought enters your mind, just allow it to float away, and come back to yourself.

4. Place yourself in a beautiful environment that's the epitome of peace to you. Maybe it's the beach or a garden. Wherever it is, imagine that you're there, and fully experience the beauty and peacefulness. Engage all of your senses.

5. Imagine that the sun is shining down on you, and as it does, imagine that you are warmed by the light. Imagine that the light from the sun begins to get stronger until it becomes thick around you, but the temperature remains pleasant. The light begins to slowly spiral around you until it becomes a bright cocoon that protects you like a strong shield against anything that might harm you. Feel how safe you are within this light.

6. From inside of the cocoon of light, picture yourself as strong and resilient. Recognize that you can handle just about anything.

7. Anytime you feel unsafe, remember this cocoon of light and allow it to spiral around you and keep you protected.

8. When you're ready, begin to come back from your med-itative state by wiggling your fingers and toes. Gently let your head roll from side to side. Open your eyes slowly and look around until you feel fully awake.

The Self-Acceptance Challenge

There's really no such thing as loving yourself "enough" or "correctly" or "perfectly." There's also no one moment when you love yourself enough and no longer have to work on it. It's something you'll work on throughout the rest of your life.

There comes a time, though, when your love for yourself turns a corner, and your life becomes better. You'll certainly notice when that happens. I know this from my own experience and the experience of others, but I can't tell you when it will happen for you.

On your journey to loving yourself more, however, here's a challenge for you. Ask yourself these questions:

If I gain fifty pounds in the next six months, can I still love myself?

If I lose my job, can I still love myself?

If I end up alone as I grow old, can I still love myself?

If you aren't sure that you can still love yourself in these circumstances, you know what you have to work on! I know it can be difficult to love yourself when you don't live up to your own expectations, but that's the task at hand. Are you up to the challenge? I'll bet you are!

Self-Compassion

Self-compassion is slightly different from self-love and self-acceptance, although it's certainly related to both of those. When you feel compassionate toward yourself, you empathize with yourself for what you've been through in life. You give yourself the same kind of understanding that you would a friend or family member you love. You forgive your mistakes and feel supportive when you fail to "perform" in the way you had hoped.

As we wrap up this book, let's capsulize some of the points we've made and think of them in terms of self-compassion:

Being kind to yourself is the number-one golden rule. Treat yourself the way you want others to treat you.

Embrace your flaws. Rather than nitpicking over every inch of your body, look at your so-called "flaws" as the things that make you unique. And if asymmetry is one of your perceived flaws, I can tell you with a high degree of certainty after seeing thousands of bodies (as a Certified Rolfer™/Massage therapist) that *no one* is 100 percent symmetrical. If your left shoulder sits closer to your ear, change your perspective on it. Maybe tell yourself that your shoulder is closer to your ear so that you can hear your spirit guides more easily.

The instant you realize you are going down the rabbit hole of self-criticism, stop and tell yourself how much you love yourself. Even if you don't believe it yet, keep telling yourself. Pretend to be someone who loves herself. How would a person who loves herself behave? How would she go about her day?

Recognize that being hard on yourself doesn't bring you happiness or success. If you're like all the rest of us, a part of you believes that if you're a slave-driver to yourself, it will cause you to get into action and do better. But the opposite is what happens. Only positive reinforcement is what propels you into action and helps you succeed. To drive this point home to yourself, write down all the times that stress and worry have brought you positive results. Can't think of anything? Me neither.

Be unconditionally present with yourself. This is a hard one. Think about being unconditionally present with another person. A beautiful thing happens. He starts to open up and trust you. You can do this with yourself as well and build trust in yourself. When you're unconditionally present with yourself, you are self-compassionate and not judgmental. You know how you feel when you're with a baby or a small child? That's the kind of feeling I'm talking about here. That's what it's like to be unconditionally, nonjudgmentally present in the moment.

Recognize that failure isn't a bad thing. It's something that happens to *everyone*. The difference is that successful people don't give up. They keep failing until they succeed.

The Attachment Syndrome

It's easy to imagine a scenario and the outcome you want. You do it all the time as you fantasize how you'd like a situation to go. But honestly, how often do any situations go the way you imagined them?

If you get attached to the outcome you want, you can become triggered when the situation doesn't go your way. For me, learning how to not be attached to the outcome was a very valuable lesson. It taught me the value of patience and that not every door I knock on will open. I simply don't have the keys to every door.

Attaching thoughts to an outcome that hasn't happened sets me up to live in the future rather than the present moment. So I have to constantly reel myself back into the present. Then, and only then, can I tell myself, "Let go, and just allow the future to unfold."

Try not to attach yourself to an outcome. What happens just might be better than you could have imagined!

MINDFUL MOMENT

There will always be someone else who is smarter, more intelligent, more beautiful, and more talented than you are. But YOU have your own talents, intelligence, and beauty, and you are 100 percent unique. No one else on the planet is exactly like you. So embrace the wonder of that. Life is short, so live it now! Don't wait another second.

BENEDICTION–
MY VISION FOR YOU

*M*y greatest hope for you is that you will learn to recognize old destructive behaviors and start to take action to change how you feel about yourself. Know that if you approach everything with kindness in your heart, good things will come to you. There will be some bumps and hurdles along the way, but trust that you are strong enough to endure them and do what you want in life. Thank you for going on this journey with me, and be sure to visit me on my website at www.fatshame.com. I'd love to hear from you!

ACKNOWLEDGMENTS

I would like to thank my daughter, Morgan, for being so patient and supportive while I wrote this book. More than anyone else on this planet, she's taught me the meaning of unconditional love and acceptance.

To my brother, Marco, thank you for always having my back and being so supportive and understanding. You've always been my rock of Gibraltar, and I'm so glad I have you.

To my soul sisters: *Jamie* for always building me up and reminding me that I am strong and capable. *Rebecca* for being my New York connection and writing teacher. And *Tara* for being the best little sister I never had and always making me laugh. Thank you all for listening and for your constant support.

To my publicist, Pia Dorer, for working so hard behind the scenes to make sure everything would work out. And to the Eschler Editing team, specifically Angela Eschler, Michele Preisendorf, and Chris Bigelow, for their help and guidance in helping bring this work to fruition, and Kathy Jenkins, my editor, for making sure my prose was polished.

Thank you to the wonderful coaches at Quantum Leap—Martha Bullen, Raia King, Danette Kubanda, Steve Harrison, and Geoffrey Berwind—you've been the wind beneath my wings, and I appreciate all you've done.

Thank you to Melanie Votaw for always believing in me, for never giving up on me, and for pushing me to work harder and do my best.

Finally, for all the people I didn't mention by name, if we have crossed paths in the last decade, you've touched my heart, and I will be forever grateful—whether our time together was a season, a reason, or a lifetime.

This book was a labor of love that took two years to come to fruition. It was worth the wait. All the best things are.

Namaste.

9 Steps
to Find Your
Happiest Weight

HAVE YOU EVER FELT LIKE YOUR SKIN WAS STRETCHED TOO TIGHT ON YOUR BODY?

HAVE YOU TRIED EVERY DIET ONLY TO END UP HEAVIER THAN WHEN YOU STARTED?

Maybe the issue isn't inside your body but rather the way you perceive your body.
Download my free guide (fatshame.com)
"9 Steps to Find Your Happiest Weight."
I look forward to hearing from you on your journey.
Remember to trust the process and yourself!

For more tips, follow me

🐦 nicolemotivate   📘 nicolemotivates   📷 nicolemotivates

or go to my website to get in touch:

www.fatshame.com

NEW!

KETO CLEANSE

21-Day
Body
Makeover

JUMPSTART YOUR
WEIGHT LOSS
WITH THE 21-DAY
KETO CLEANSE

You can learn more about the
cleanse on my website:
www.fatshame.com

ABOUT THE AUTHOR

Nicole Black is an author and entrepreneur. She is also cofounder and former CEO of Renaud's Patisserie & Bistro in Santa Barbara and Los Angeles.

A native of Southern California, she currently resides in Santa Barbara with her daughter. When she isn't working to promote her story of getting healthy from the inside out, she enjoys travel, yoga, Pilates, and chasing dragonflies.

For more information or to follow her, please go to her website, www.fatshame.com; she would love to hear from you.

Manufactured by Amazon.ca
Bolton, ON